ch

)

Language

Structures

in

Contrast

LANGUAGE STRUCTURES

IN

CONTRAST

Robert J. Di Pietro

Georgetown University

NEWBURY HOUSE PUBLISHERS

Rowley, Massachusetts

LANGUAGE STRUCTURES IN CONTRAST

ISBN 912066 11 3

Library of Congress Catalogue Card Number   71–142801

First Printing: August 1971

Printed in the United States.

for Elisa

INTRODUCTION

Contrastive linguistics was born of classroom experience. Every teacher of a foreign language knows, and every student of a foreign language soon finds out, that the native language of the learner interferes in specific and predictable ways at each new step in acquiring a second language. The teacher's bag of tricks consists mainly of ways to overcome that interference. If he knows that there is a widespread cognate relationship between *r*'s in the target language and in the native language, he will be on guard against a tendency to interpret one in terms of the other. As between English and languages with a tapped *r* this might involve his noting also that a *d* or a *t* between vowels in rapid speech in English tends to be produced in much the same way as the desired pronunciation of the *r*, and using that as a bridge.

For a bag of tricks to be transformed into a technique calls for a set of principles and a steady search, language by language, for the trouble spots.

The teacher or the textbook writer must be thoroughly familiar with the structures of the languages to be compared and must know of enough linguistic theory to know *about* what he knows. In one language a meaning may be conveyed by a particle, in another by word order. In one a question may be signaled by a function word, in another by intonation. A stress may do here what a gender change may do elsewhere. To be prepared for collisions, we need to know the road. Contrastive linguistics is the discipline that charts it.

If comparing two languages had no purpose except to make it easier for speakers of one to learn the other, a catalog of teaching devices would probably suffice. The compiler would need to possess the riches of both in order to make his compilation, but the teacher and the student could do with less. This might have been enough yesterday; it is no longer enough today. Learning a language merely to use it is too costly for those who may never have the opportunity to go abroad or to mingle with different ethnic groups at home. Language teaching is on the defensive nowadays, and some of its defenses are none too strong. Surely one of the strongest, equal to that of gaining empathy with another culture, is insight into the nature of language itself. The experience of learning, even imperfectly, the system by which other human beings code their meanings is one that any student will be the poorer for having missed. We can do much better than we have done in giving our students this enrichment. The foundation for it is contrastive linguistics. The teacher and the student need it as much as the compiler of lists and the maker of texts.

While contrastive linguistics draws on linguistic theory and contributes to it, no allegiance is owed by it to any particular theory. The first systematic contrastive studies were made a decade ago when structuralism still held sway, and some recent critics have identified the two and have argued that comparing one structure with another has little value in teaching. Since the habit theory has to be discarded, the devices to form new habits must go with them. This notion has been ably refuted by T. Grant Brown, who points out that what we know about interference is empirical knowledge and does not depend on theories, which themselves fail precisely to the extent that they are unable to account for interference. "The only effect on interference and habit theory," he writes of the new theories of language, "is the redefinition of terms to agree with recent developments in linguistics and psychology."*

Professor Di Pietro keeps the baby and changes the bath. His book brings contrastive linguistics up to date by adjusting it to current linguistic theory and the advances in other fields that have been affected by it. Our ideas

*"In Defense of Pattern Practise," *Language Learning* 19.200 (1969).

about characteristics shared among languages—and hence, as students learn one on the basis of another, our ideas of transfer between them—are deepened by the understanding of universals. Our vacillation over how much can be inferred about learning a second language from the way one learned a first is steadied by a grasp of language in relation to cognitive growth. And our powers of comparison are augmented by familiarity with the levels of deep and surface structure.

This is not exclusively a text for language practitioners by linguistic theorists. It is equally a text for theorists by practitioners. There is much that theory can do to improve application. But application is the proof of theory. The professionals on both sides need one another, and we have here a gathering point.

DWIGHT BOLINGER
Harvard University
Cambridge, Massachusetts

PREFACE

The preface to a book is often the last part of it to be written. And for good reason. No matter how carefully the author may plan his book, the details of its contents have a way of lending their own color to the composite whole. If the preface had been worked out before the central chapters, it would most certainly have included a claim that the book is a practical guide to contrasting languages. The student of language would surely appreciate having something practical, especially with regard to linguistics. Yet there is a danger that, in making things practical, we also make them superficial. Besides, practicality, like beauty, depends very much on the one who is seeking it. Nonetheless, the book *is* practical. But not in the sense that minutiae are handled with simplistic invariance. There is little emphasis on orthodoxy in finding solutions to contrastive problems. Moreover, even though the linguistic approach is strongly transformational, there is no dogmatism in it. Instead, the effort has been to encourage the reader to think creatively about diversities and similarities in languages. All of the illustrations and explanations are offered with this singular goal in mind.

Extent of Coverage

The coverage, although it may seem quite extensive, is limited in some ways. Among the aspects of language not treated are accent, pitch, and tone. Some noteworthy proposals for handling such matters in a transformational grammar have been recently suggested but have not been sufficiently generalized to languages other than English so that they are suitable for use in a text on contrastive analysis (see, for example, Chomsky and Halle 1968). The reader will also note that phonology is not taken up until both syntax and semantics have been discussed. This arrangement is in keeping with the view that the primary function of phonology is to convert underlying grammatical structure into patterns of sound. No attempt has been made to contrast cultural systems. Such a task would require the dedication of an entire book in order to be meaningful.

Adaptation

The book is intended for use in a course on linguistics for students who, having had some introduction to the field, now wish to consider the ways in which linguistic theory can be applied to the practical matter of contrasting languages. Although the initial chapters do not presuppose much previous training in linguistics, the text, taken as a whole, is not for beginners. Instead, the intention has been to present some of the contemporary themes of linguistics to the advanced student who eventually may have the need to implement them in language teaching or in designing new instructional programs.

The book's eight chapters are of a length to be covered comfortably within the time span of a regular college semester course. The problems supplied at the ends of the chapters are perhaps best done as outside work and then discussed in class. A preliminary version of the text was used at Georgetown University in this way. Another useful technique is to have students submit a weekly résumé of one of the readings listed in the bibliography. These résumés can be reproduced for later distribution to the remainder of the class. Requirements for the course in contrastive linguistics at Georgetown include also a brief oral report from each student on some area of contrast between two languages. Professor Larry Selinker, who teaches a similar course at the University of Washington, Seattle, uses another approach. He prefers to have the reports prepared in written form and then distributed widely—even outside the university. If the book is to be used in conjunction with other texts, the teacher may wish to forego these techniques. In any event, readings in both sociolinguistics and psycholinguistics will supplement this book in significant ways, permitting coverage of three important aspects of language: its formal structure, its use in society, and its psychological implications.

Some Useful Information about Contrastive Studies

Contrastive analysis is actively pursued in many places. Perhaps the most prominent in this respect is the University of Michigan. It was at its Ann Arbor campus that the journal *Language Learning* was founded and continues to publish many papers on contrastive analysis. Robert Lado was Director of its English Language Institute when he wrote *Linguistics across Cultures,* to date the only general text in the field. Yao Shen, a faculty member of the university, has long contributed articles to *Language Learning* dealing with both theory and the practical application of contrastive analysis. Other linguists, such as Charles Fries and Kenneth Pike, provided important guidance with regard to the underlying linguistic theory.

Indiana University is another center of contrastive studies. Especially noteworthy is its series of studies in Uralic and Altaic languages, with emphasis on the contrasts between English and Hungarian by Nemser (1961), Nemser and Juhasz (1964), and Kiefer (1967).

For several years, Professor Selinker of the University of Washington has directed his students in preparing a series of exercises in contrastive linguistics. These unpublished exercises are available in reproduced form and cover many aspects of linguistic theory as it applies to contrasting languages.

Everett Kleinjans, with the aid of Kenneth Jackson and Randal Whitman, all of the University of Hawaii, organized the Pacific Conference on Contrastive Linguistics and Language Universals (Honolulu, Hawaii, January 11-16, 1971). The purpose of the conference was to promote cooperation between East and West on matters of theory and application. One sign of the recent developments in the field is the incorporation of language universals as part of the major focus of attention.

Georgetown University, Washington, D.C., is the home university of the author and the scene of a major recent (1968) effort to further studies in contrastive analysis. The nineteenth annual Round Table Conference at that university dealt in its entirety with contrastive linguistics. Proceedings of the meeting are published as monograph no. 21 in the *Georgetown Series on Linguistics and Language Study* (Alatis 1968).

It is impossible to mention all of the linguists and language teachers who have been active in contrastive studies either directly or indirectly. Robert Politzer of Stanford University, for example, has written a series of books for teachers in which contrastive analysis occupies a basic position (see Politzer 1960; Politzer and Staubach 1961; Politzer 1968). Methodologists such as Rivers (1968) and Finocchiaro (1964) assume a central importance for contrastive data.

The Center for Applied Linguistics of Washington, D.C., has long sustained vital interest in contrastive studies. One of its early publications, Cárdenas's *Introducción a una comparación fonológica del español y del inglés* (1960), served for many years as a practical guide for teachers of Spanish in the United States. They have also sponsored a number of bibliographies on contrastive analysis: Gage (1961), Ferguson and Stewart (1963), and Hammer and Rice (1965). Between 1960 and 1965, the Center contracted with the United States Office of Education to produce a major series of contrastive studies of English with the five commonly taught foreign languages in the United States: French, German, Italian, Russian, and Spanish. Teams of linguists were organized for each set of languages. The first to appear was the German study by Moulton (1962) and Kufner (1962). Robert Stockwell joined with Donald Bowen and John Martin to produce the Spanish-English set in 1965 (see Stockwell and Bowen 1965; and Stockwell, Bowen, and Martin 1965). That same year, the Italian-English study was also published (Agard and Di Pietro 1965, 1965a), although it had been completed in manuscript form some three years earlier. The Russian-English and French-English volumes were never published but have been made available through the auspices of the Educational Resources Information Center (ERIC) of the United States Office of Education (see Lampach and Martinet, unpublished, and Gage, unpublished). The intent of the series, then under the general editorship of Charles Ferguson, was to provide an aid to the teacher of each of the five foreign languages in the United States.

Now under the leadership of John Lotz, the Center has extended its interest in contrastive analysis to lesser known languages, viz., to Choctaw, Navajo, Papago (Ohannessian and Gage 1969). Both Lotz and William Nemser have worked extensively on Eastern European languages. A survey of the Center's activities can be found in Nemser (1970).

An effort to improve dissemination of contrastive materials has been recently announced. Papers dealing with either theory or application of contrastive analysis may now be submitted to the Project for Information Dissemination in Linguistics, Center for Applied Linguistics, 1717 Massachusetts Avenue, N.W., Washington, D.C. 20036. These papers will be made available either in the form of microfiche or microfilm at modest prices, and each new title will be listed both in *Foreign Language Annals* (a journal published by the American Council on the Teaching of Foreign Languages) and in the *Publications of the Modern Language Association (PMLA)*.

Interest in contrastive analysis among Europeans has grown considerably. The tenth triennial congress of the *Fédération internationale de professeurs de langues vivantes* (held in Zagreb, Yugoslavia, April 5 to 9, 1968) resulted in a resolution to include reports on contrastive projects as part of its regular meetings and a list of recommendations as to how contrastive analysis should be done (see chapter 1). The following year, a panel of the Second International Congress of Applied Linguistics (held in Cambridge, England, September 8 to 12, 1969) was dedicated to contrastive linguistics.

Among European centers of contrastive study is the one at the Technical University of Stuttgart. It is under the direction of Gerhard Nickel and bears as a title the acronym *PAKS (Projekt für Angewandte Kontrastive Sprachwissenschaft)*. The staff of *PAKS* prepares and distributes progress reports on various aspects of its work in contrasting German with English. An additional service performed by *PAKS* is the collection and dissemination of bibliographical information on contrastive studies done throughout the world.

A Serbo-Croatian and English contrastive project has been undertaken at the university in Zagreb, Yugoslavia. Director of the project is Rudolf Filipović. Since its inception in 1968, the number of Yugoslav linguists actively engaged in the project has grown to approximately thirty. As in the case of *PAKS,* workpapers are duplicated and distributed from time to time.

Other East European countries have begun to establish centers where contrastive studies can be conducted systematically: Romania, Poland, Hungary, and Czechoslovakia. In each case, English is one of the languages involved. There is every reason to believe that such centers will continue to appear throughout the world as individual countries recognize the need to improve instruction in some language of wider communication which is not natively spoken by the population.

Acknowledgments

The author holds a debt of gratitude to many. First of all, I would like to thank Vincenzina Giallo Di Pietro, my wife, for her unwavering support throughout the writing of the book.

Deserving of special mention among professional colleagues is Professor

Dwight Bolinger of Harvard who not only gave needed encouragement at difficult times but was also most kind in going through the manuscript and offering many useful suggestions. Professor Ursula Oomen-Mantell should be singled out among my colleagues at Georgetown who read preliminary drafts and graciously gave of their valuable time in suggesting revisions. Professor Frederick J. Bosco was helpful in his critical reading of the last chapter. The many Georgetown students who contributed perhaps more than they realize through their classroom comments cannot be thanked individually, but their presence is felt on almost every page.

ROBERT J. DI PIETRO

CONTENTS

xvii

Chapter 1

DEVELOPMENTS IN

CONTRASTIVE ANALYSIS

The purpose of this book is to relate aspects of contemporary linguistic theory to the contrasting of languages. While a contrastive study is motivated chiefly by the foreign language teacher's need to uncover important areas of difference between the language he is teaching and that of his students, the value of contrastive analysis as a way to evaluate the postulations and claims of linguistic theory itself should not be overlooked. To better understand the technical discussions wherever they occur in the book, the reader may wish to consult a general textbook in introductory linguistics. Several are listed in the bibliography.

The book has been arranged so that all essentials of linguistic theory, background, and practice are presented in the first three chapters. In the present chapter, for example, some basic linguistic notions are discussed, and a brief survey of important developments in contrastive analysis (hereafter abbreviated CA) is provided. The second chapter, "Theory and Procedures," is devoted to an explanation of how CA can be done and what justification there is for it within linguistic theory. Detailed explanation and illustrations from actual languages are given in chapters 4, 5, 6, and 7. The reader who is interested only in general principles may wish to read the first three chapters in detail and then skip the next four. Working through the problems given in chapters 4 through 7 will provide the reader with an understanding of contrastive procedures in their various forms. Chapter 8 is devoted to the implications of CA for a theory of second language instruction. Specifically in chapter 8, guidelines are given for the interpretation of contrastive data in various kinds of instructional strategies.

1.1 General Remarks

Neither linguists nor language teachers who have had any exposure to linguistics will be overly surprised at the definition of CA as the method whereby the differences between two (or, more rarely, among more than two) languages are made explicit. Yet, to fully understand the implications of this definition plunges us deeply into some very basic matters about language description and the formulation of linguistic theories. Under the heading of descriptive linguistics, investigators have amassed and continue to amass data about the structure of particular languages. To analyze these data, they employ tools which have been developed within the general field of linguistics and which are subject to reformulation or even total rejection as new aspects of language are discovered. The phoneme, for example, has been a very useful tool for describing the sounds of a language. It loses its explanatory force, however, if we go beyond the consideration of a language's sounds as patterns in themselves and try to understand how a language utilizes sounds to interpret the grammar that lies beneath them. To cite a classical example, phonemic theory has never been able to explain the medial flap [r] of English words like *latter* and *ladder* which under different phonological conditions and grammatical considerations is connected with either [t] or [d]. For further discussion, see Bloch (1941). Chomsky and Halle's *Sound Pattern of English* (1968) clearly demonstrates the need to go beyond autonomous phonemics to considerations of how grammatical elements are realized as sounds. For Chomsky and Halle, as for many other contemporary linguists, much more explanatory power is derived from systematic phonemics, in which each phoneme represents a family of grammatically interrelated sounds, such as /I/, the second vowel of *divine* and *divinity*, and the /E/ of *serene* and *serenity*, or the /A/ of *profane* and *profanity*. Most importantly, contemporary phonology has moved away from considering sound units in a language as the main purpose of the study and has concentrated, instead, on the explanations or rules of how strings of sounds can be generated. The explanations are usually in terms of features which compose each sound complex.

One of the most important of recent developments in linguistics is the revival of interest in language universals. Whereas earlier speculations about essential linguistic properties were hampered by a lack of empirical data and an inclination to follow closely a Greco-Latin mold, the recent efforts have had the benefit of a rather large storehouse of information about the world's languages. Moreover, linguists are better prepared theoretically to postulate language universals. As we shall see in later chapters, the assumption that there are universal constraints in languages is basic to the implementation of CA. In a very real sense, CA is reduced to nothing more than an exercise in taxonomy without the notion that the specifics of each language reflect, in some way or another, universal linguistic properties. Whatever our interests in linguistics, we have to agree that the grammar of individual languages must contribute, in some way, to the grammatical theory of all languages.

Even if we were forced to rationalize in the absence of extensive empirical evidence from actual languages, as did the early linguists and the philosophers who preceded them, we would still have to conclude that human languages share many properties. Below the superficial differences of race, every man has the genetic endowment of his species. This endowment includes language ability. It can be demonstrated that every society of man has language. Without it, communication could not be so complex, and human society would become something less than human. Despite variations in detail due to environmental factors and historical change, the particular languages of man are alike in many essential ways. Regardless of where he may live—desert, jungle, arctic waste—man must name things, describe states of being and action, express acceptance or refusal, ask questions, and discuss causes and effects, to name but a few matters of fundamental importance to man's social life. In addition to these needs of communication, man's logic leads him to place some universal constraints on the form of his language. To avoid repetition of full nouns and to interrelate noun references, he devises grammatical forms to substitute for names of things (such as the use of pronouns in English or simple contextual rules in Japanese). He may use grammatical markers or adhere to positional rules in order to explicate the relationships between the objects of his discourse.

Man has found an economy of expression by utilizing a limited number of sounds to express a limitless number of meanings. Because his stock of sound features is always smaller than the number of syntactic and semantic elements which they convey, man introduces various types of redundancy into his language whereby certain parts of the message are reiterated. In the English sentence *He goes,* for example, the inflection of the verb reiterates the third person reference conveyed by the pronoun *he.* To overcome potential ambiguities or simply to avoid monotony, each of man's languages has ways of varying the form of a message. The active-passive relationship of English

4 LANGUAGE STRUCTURES IN CONTRAST

operates only with regard to agent. Thus, *The houses were painted by John* and *John painted the houses* are related because *John* is the agent in both cases. Another sentence, *The houses were painted by noon,* has no counterpart with *noon* as subject because *noon* is not an agent.

As we consider linguistic universals, it is extremely important to bear in mind that communicative needs and logical restraints do not operate to produce exactly the same results. In other words, even if man does feel a universal need to name things, there is no reason that he should concretize this need in the specific ways in which it is done in English, German, French, or any other language. Many forces, both linguistic and nonlinguistic, work in shaping the particular grammar of each language. Perhaps the most accurate statement that one could make in this respect is that the universally shared characteristics of human language stem from man's genetic endowment as man (Lenneberg 1967) and that a certain amount of variation in language is due to adaptation and change. Strong support for this viewpoint is the fact that none of man's languages is rendered inaccessible to a human learner because of that learner's racial or ethnic background. We are all endowed with the necessary equipment to learn each other's languages. This equipment has been termed the "language acquisition device" by some linguists and psychologists.

The supposition that human languages all share a number of essential features is crucial to achieving a level of adequacy in CA. If there were no such sharing of both a general framework and a number of grammatical processes, there would be no point of departure for the contrastive statements to be made. The alternative to positing universals in CA is a list of contrasting paradigms and autonomous descriptive statements with no interrelating of the languages being contrasted. It is, unfortunately, a matter of record that most of the existent CAs have not been made in terms of explicit universals and, as a result, have not reached a high level of explanatory adequacy.

Before we can fully understand the meaning of adequacy in the context of CA, we shall have to consider some basic matters about particular and universal grammar. Briefly put, universal grammar is an abstraction containing all processes and forms vital to the general theory of language. So far, we have only hinted at the nature of these processes and forms, but their importance will be made clear as our discussion of CA progresses.

Speculation as to the nature of universal grammar follows, theoretically, the investigation of particular grammars. The procedure is to describe a number of specific languages and then extrapolate what is shared. Once an understanding is reached of shared properties, these properties can be correlated with what is known about man's cognitive processes.

In this way, the postulation of language universals rests both on observed data and on correlation with supposed physiological limitations. (Later on, we shall see how a universal view of language organization accommodates three major components: semantic, syntactic, and phonological.)

Even in its rudimentary form, viewing language from the standpoint of universals readily allows for symbolizing the similarities and diversities among languages. If all languages share universals, then any differences are to be found in the ways these universals are realized in particular grammars. If a given language x resembles language y more than it does language z, it is because either the accident of history or membership in the same language family has led to significant similarities in the realization of abstract universals. The importance of universals for CA is felt even in those cases where we are forced to discuss the absence of some linguistic feature. Nonoccurrence is meaningless if we cannot admit the existence of that feature elsewhere. In other words, if we did not see some underlying universal whereby a feature is realized somewhere, its absence would not be noticed by us.

The four criteria for evaluating linguistic descriptions (completeness, accuracy, explicitness, and simplicity) cited in the literature on transformational grammar (see, for example, Bach 1964) are meaningful only if the distinction between universal and particular grammar is accepted. Otherwise, it is doubtful that these criteria could be met, especially that of completeness.

The view of language organization presented in chapter 3 incorporates the notion that there are distinct levels of structuring to grammar. Elements that function at a very basic (or deep) level of structure may be found to underlie any number of different elements standing at less basic (surface) levels. Rules for the formation of active and passive sentences, for example, are often used to convey identical basic grammatical elements despite the different surface arrangements that emerge. It is important to keep clear the distinction between deep and surface structure on one hand and universal and particular grammar on the other. Languages tend to show greater diversity in their surface structures and less diversity as deep levels are probed. While it might be proposed that the deepest of levels is comprised of universal elements, features will also be found at more nearly surface levels of structure which can be said to derive from universal processes (cf. Bach 1965).

1.2 Transfer and Interference: Psychological Implications

In talking about language, linguists devise various techniques which are then open to psychological interpretation. The view of language in the present book is rule oriented. That is to say, the grammar of each language is interpreted as consisting of a set of formalized explanations which, when put into operation, yield the sentences of that language. These explanations, or rules, are ordered so that the progression is from the general to the specific. For example, the rule that places the subject before the predicate in English declarative sentences is more general than any rule dealing with the specifics of either the subject or the predicate.

Paralleling the view of grammar as a set of rules is the psychological interpretation of language as rule-oriented behavior. With this interpretation, it can be said that the speakers of a language must utilize the rules of that language in order to produce and understand its sentences. Thus the speaker of English accepts the sentence *I am happy about it* as being English just as the monolingual speaker of German accepts *Das freut mich* as a sentence in German. Whenever the monolingual speaker of German hears the sentence *I am happy about it,* he rejects it as being a sentence in his language just as the monolingual speaker of English would reject *Das freut mich* as an English sentence. As part of the process of converting the speaker of one language into a learner of the other, we equip him with the necessary rules to be able to produce and understand the sentences of that language as well as those of his own. Of course, his ability to apply these rules depends to a large extent on the type of instruction we give him, his memory limitations, his interest, and many other factors. At any rate, it is safe to say that if he has properly learned the rules of the other language, he will be able to apply them. Whenever he has not learned the rules, he will have to revert to those of his native language or to those of other languages he knows. (The psychological effects of knowing more than one language on the learning of a new one are evident but are not well understood. Language teachers often observe a tendency among some students to confuse the language they are studying with others studied previously or concurrently.) The process of interpreting the particular grammar of one language in terms of another is called *transfer.* The mistakes that result from this process are said to be due to *interference.* Jakobovits (1970) discusses the notion of transfer and its effects in some detail for the language teacher.

Studies of interference have been conducted by both psychologists and linguists. Eugene J. Brière (1968) reports on an experiment conducted to establish a hierarchy of learning difficulties in phonology. (See chapter 8 for further discussion of hierarchies of difficulties.) A stimulus-response model was used which was not rule oriented. The difficulty of learning, Brière concluded, depends on whether the systems represented are convergent or divergent. It is, however, extremely difficult, if not impossible, to classify any of the parameters as convergent or divergent. Brière feels that the linguistic parameters are rarely the same as the psychological ones. If in practice such is the case, it should not be so theoretically. For our linguistic rules to be realistic, they must be reconcilable with psychological correlates. If we fail to find these correlates, the reasons for our failure may well derive from an over-compartmentalized view of language. Brière's experiment is restricted to the sound system, with no reference to the syntax and semantics which underlie it. Yet it can be argued that errors of pronunciation committed by the learner can be explained only by taking into account the entire structure of language. The sound patterns of a language do not exist independently of their meanings—unless, of course, the intention of the speaker is to utter only nonsense syllables. Moreover, errors may result either in areas of great similarity (convergence) or great diversity (divergence). For example, if French-speaking students of English can be observed to use *library* to mean *bookstore* (on the model of French *librairie*), it may well be a result of the similarity between the French and the English words. The ways in which similarity and diversity between languages promote interference are still open to investigation. (For another study of interference, see Selinker 1966).

Not every error made by the language learner has its origins in the contrasts between native language and language being learned. Some errors are due to factors such as memory retention and the type of instruction used by the teacher. Order of presentation is yet another very significant factor. After all, it is difficult for a student to make a mistake in the use of the subjunctive in a given language until he is made aware that such a grammatical item exists. If the goal of grammatical presentation is to enable the student to say more in the language being studied by him, the teacher should be aware of its undesirable side effects: to know more grammar is to be able to make more mistakes. (Perhaps a modicum of fatalism is necessary in language teaching! Even in learning how to swim, the student is bound to swallow some water.)

Other errors made in language learning are due to overgeneralization. Take for example, the case of noun pluralization in English. It is quite possible that both a speaker of Chinese and a speaker of Spanish will make the same error in pluralizing English nouns at some point in the course of instruction, saying *mans for *men* or *childs for *children*. Both learners will tend to over-extend the domain of the noun-pluralizing rule by the process of analogy: *boy* → *boys; bag* → *bags; room* → *rooms;* and so *man* → *mans*. (Extending the domain of a rule beyond its grammatical limits by analogy is apparently a universal tendency in second-language, as well as in first-language, learning.) Contrasting the rules of Spanish and Chinese with those of English does reveal some important differences between the former two. Whereas Spanish turns out to have rules of pluralization which utilize sibilants suffixed to noun stems in a manner similar to English, Chinese has no such rules. In the case of Chinese, we must search higher in the particular rules than we would in Spanish if we are to understand what happens to expressions of plurality. Not only are rules producing plural markers by suffixation absent in Chinese, but we find that Chinese does not share with Spanish and English many redundancy rules requiring the use of plural markers. Although the Spanish speaker is faced with less novelty than the Chinese speaker in learning English, both are likely to overextend the domain of some of its rules in a similar fashion.

Until much more is known about both the linguistic rules and their psychological correlates, it will be impossible to predict exactly *when* errors will occur in the learning process. We cannot overemphasize the point that much depends on the particular strategy of instruction and the manner in which the rules are presented. The information yielded by a CA is of great value not only to the teacher in planning his personal approach but also to the methodologist in writing materials for instruction. But CA is not a panacea. While the teacher needs contrastive information on which to base his course of instruction, there is nothing in that information which endorses a particular method of instruction. Finally, CA can be of value even to the theoretical linguist who seeks some support for his theories of language.

1.3 Implications of Psychological Research for CA

Although the specifics of linguistic theories have not been correlated very closely with psychological and physiological research on human speech, recent work such as that of the psychologist Eric Lenneberg is opening new areas of potential interpolation (cf. his book *Biological Foundations of Language,* 1967). Lenneberg sees a parallelism between the child's physical development and his acquisition of language. The normal child is genetically endowed with the ability to learn a language. This ability is expressed in the form of particular language behavior as the child matures physically. One of the implications of Lenneberg's research is that there is a set of underlying language capabilities shared by all humans regardless of the particular language they happen to speak. Any explanation of the unique elements found in particular languages, then, would necessarily entail a consideration of how they stem from language universals. These universals can be thought of, at least in part, as correlations to biologically determined cognitive processes.

The stimulus and response theories of habit formation that have motivated much of audiolingual instruction in the past thirty years are not overly concerned with the mental organization underlying language production. Instead, language acquisition is looked upon as the formation of habits through the use of selected stimuli. These stimuli condition the desired responses in the learner.   As the learner is exposed to increasing numbers of different stimuli, he builds new responses and expands his "inventory."   Wilga Rivers (1964) has an extensive discussion of such theories and their applications in language teaching.

There are several limitations to habit formation theories.   First of all, it is not clear that every act of speech is triggered by some stimulus: Certainly I am not reacting to any overt stimulus as I sit at my typewriter and write these words.   More importantly, little opportunity is given to discuss the universal framework of grammar which gives form to the patterns of language. This is not to imply that the nativistic theories of psychologists like Lenneberg are above criticism.   There are many problems inherent in postulating "innate" features of human cognition and the universals of language which supposedly arise from them.   Despite this fact, the theoretical foundations of CA are strengthened significantly by any effort to seek psychological and physiological correlates to the systems of grammar that are contrasted.

Regardless of the psychological theory of language learning to be adopted, important differences can be observed between the child's acquisition of language and that of an older person who is learning a language other than his own.   The child must acquire the rudiments of human communication via language along with the specifics of the language or languages spoken around him.   The adult, on the other hand, has already acquired the essentials of language communication as well as one or more particular language.   (We should not exclude the possibility that the child may grow up in bilingual surroundings.   It remains to be proven that the bilingual child's acquisition of language is qualitatively different from that of the monolingual child.) Whatever new language the adult may learn, he will inevitably make comparisons with the language or languages he already knows.

1.4 Background Notes

Acquaintance with the background of contrastive studies can be useful in understanding the present state of the art.   We shall consider only those developments which have some theoretical relevance today.   Principally, CA is a product of linguistic science during approximately the last 25 years.   Although published work that could be called contrastive with regard to languages before the decade of the 1940s is sporadic, some notable efforts from earlier times should be mentioned.   As early as 1892, a renowned philological specialist in Romance languages, Charles H. Grandgent, published his *German and English Sounds*.   Two years later, another noted philologist, Wilhelm Viëtor, had already produced his third edition of *Elemente der Phonetik des Deutschen, Englischen und Französischen* in Leipzig, a city which was a great center of activity in language study during the nineteenth century. The French phonetician, Paul Passy, followed in 1906 with his *Petite phonétique comparée des principales langues européennes.* Many linguists of the Prague school became interested in CA. One of the principal figures in that movement, Matesius, wrote a CA of English and Czech in 1926.

Perhaps the first sign that a momentum was building in the contrastive study of languages came in 1933 with Yuen Ren Chao's "A Preliminary Study of English Intonation (with American Variants) and Its Chinese Equivalents" (in *Studies Presented to Ts'ai Yuan P'ei on His Sixty-Fifth Birthday* published by the Academia Sinica in Peiping). Only eight years later, Benjamin Lee Whorf (1941) was able to write the following prophetic words:

> Much progress has been made in classifying the languages of the earth into genetic families, each having descent from a single precursor, and in tracing such developments through time. The result is called "comparative linguistics." Of even greater importance for the future technology of thought is what might be called "contrastive linguistics." This plots the outstanding differences among tongues—in grammar, logic, and general analysis of experience.

In the years since Whorf, the theoretical implications of CA were to come to its applications in foreign language teaching and the study of bilingualism. Without making specific reference to the term, the groundwork was laid for the pedagogical use of CA in 1948 by David Reed, Robert Lado, and Yao Shen. Their article "The Importance of the Native Language in Foreign Language Learning" appeared in the first issue of *Language Learning,* a journal which was to become the forum for voicing opinions and research on many aspects of applying CA to language teaching. (It is often difficult to trace the origins of ideas. Henry Sweet had suggested comparing languages for the purpose of teaching much before the work of Reed, Lado, and Shen. Actual attempts to do so did not, however, come until later.)

The first extensive application of structural linguistics to CA was to be in connection with investigation of bilingualism. A large part of Uriel Weinreich's pace-setting study, *Languages in Contact* (first published in 1953) provided a conceptual framework for understanding the ways in which languages in bilingual situations may affect each other phonetically, grammatically, and lexically. To describe the negative influence of one language on another in the bilingual context, Weinreich made extensive use of the term "interference." To lay the groundwork for interpreting bilingual speech, C. C. Fries and K. L. Pike (1949) collaborated on an article entitled "Co-existent Phonemic Systems."

The next milestone in the development of CA as a theory was Zellig Harris's article "Transfer Grammar" (1954). It is Harris who should be credited with adopting a rule-oriented approach to language structure. The formulas which he proposed for contrasting languages can be summed up as follows:

$$R_{sl} + (R_{tl} - R_{sl}) = R_{tl}$$

i.e., the rules of the target language are obtainable by adding to the rules of the source language those of the target language which are not to be found in the source language. In addition to the notion that languages could be thought of as sets of rules, there is the assumption in Harris's work that some of the rules are likely to be shared by both languages involved in the contrastive procedure. If this assumption is extended far enough, it becomes possible to think of some of the rules as being shared by all languages, thereby being candidates for universal status. Harris, of course, did not go that far.

The first and, up to now, the only book devoted totally to the methods of CA is Robert Lado's *Linguistics across Cultures*, published in 1957. Like Weinreich's book, the orientation was strictly that of structural linguistics. Such an orientation was to be understood since structuralism was in its prime at the time. Evidence that the applicational value of CA was rapidly outdistancing efforts to keep apace of linguistic foundations can be found in the publication of another book that same year which was to revolutionize linguistics: Noam Chomsky's *Syntactic Structures*. The many reformulations that came about in linguistic theory because of Chomsky could not be immediately applied in CA, with the result that theory and application to language theory grew further and further apart.

At least one linguist was not reticent to try out the new transformational grammar in CA—even in the last years of the 1950s. Robert Stockwell, a specialist in both theoretical linguistics and language teaching, applied the theory as it was then formulated in a contrastive study of English and Tagalog. His work was never published, but it was circulated widely and referred to often in the literature. Then, in 1960, Paul Schachter also applied the principles of transformational grammar, together with Harris's transfer formulas in his Ph.D. dissertation, *A Contrastive Analysis of English and Pangasinan*. Other dissertations dealing with transformational grammar and CA began to appear after Schachter's. William Dingwall (1964) proposed a number of rules by which the contrastive procedure could be formalized.

The most ambitious effort to date in CA is represented by the three sets of contrastive studies involving English with German, Spanish, and Italian, published by the University of Chicago Press (Moulton, 1962; Kufner, 1962; Stockwell and Bowen, 1965; Stockwell, Bowen, and Martin, 1965; Agard and

Di Pietro, 1965, 1965a). They were done at a time of great upheaval in linguistic theory. Transformational grammar was winning more and more terrain from structuralism. Certainly, the structural approach would be soon outdated. It was, however, the form of linguistics best known to teachers of foreign languages, for whom the series was intended. On the other hand, transformational grammar was developing rapidly and providing more and more tools of language analysis. The record shows that the authors of the English-German and English-Italian studies chose to remain within a structural framework while Stockwell, Bowen, and Martin struck out in the new directions indicated by transformational grammar. Three years later, Stockwell (1968) would make a plea for continued interest in the English-Spanish study despite the difficulty in understanding the technical aspects of the work.

The reader should be advised that the interpretation of any CA, whatever its theoretical orientation, involves an historical perspective. An axiom well worth remembering is that a CA is only as good as the linguistic theory on which it is founded. As theories change, new avenues of contrast present themselves. If there are discrepancies in the theories themselves, these discrepancies will be painfully evident in application to CA.

As an indication of the directions in which contrastive studies are likely to move, we summarize the ten recommendations made by the *Fédération internationale de professeurs de langues vivantes* (at a meeting in Yugoslavia in 1968):

1. In spite of the unsettled state of research on linguistic theory, CA should be continued because of its value for teaching.

2. CA should not be limited to major world languages.

3. CA should be initiated with primary regard to theoretical implications and secondarily for its pedagogical worth.

4. CA should be considered only one of various pedagogical aids for the teacher.

5. CA should be undertaken beyond the sentence level into discourse structure, in semantics, and on the sociocultural and psycholinguistic levels.

6. CA should be undertaken in the study of stages of native language development in children.

7. In phonology, CA should be based on articulatory features.

8. CA must be done using homogeneous criteria or models (i.e., using one descriptive model throughout).

9. At future meetings of the Federation, there should be representatives who are working with advanced theoretical subjects relevant to language teaching.

10. The possibility should be considered of establishing an international symposium on theoretical and applied CA.

In subsequent chapters of this book, the reader will find that at least six of these recommendations have been considered seriously. Sociocultural and psycholinguistic data are too varied and complex to be treated adequately in a volume which is devoted to the treatment of linguistic contrasts. As for discourse structure, much more theoretical ground must be gained before a CA of language-specific patterns can be profitably attempted. Finally, the last two recommendations, although we support them, are not pertinent to the technical aspects of CA.

1.5 Topics for Discussion

1. Picture yourself as a traveler in a country where you know nothing of the language. What needs of communication would you consider to be vital to you, regardless of the cultural differences, to get through the day?

2. Language learning can be interpreted as the formation of habits or the learning of rules. Would either interpretation support or deny the concept of transfer? Discuss.

3. Give some examples that have come to your attention of possible overgeneralization in the learning of foreign languages.

4. What are some of the factors involved in the strategy of instruction that might affect the prediction of student errors?

1.6 Notes

1. The notion that interference does not stem uniquely from differences between native and target languages was expressed as early as 1962 by Yao Shen. Even similarity in language structure can cause errors on the part of the students (see Shen 1962).

2. Dingwall (1964) gives ample illustration of how transformational grammar can be utilized in contrasting languages.

3. A noted tendency among transformational theorists in recent years is to deemphasize the differences among languages, relegating them to surface layers. The theoretical position taken in this book is that both similarities and differences must be carefully mapped out if we are to gain any insight into the universals of human language and to cast the contrastive statements in their proper perspective.

4. Although the quest for universals in language was not one of the major concerns of American structuralists in the 1930s and 1940s, it was never declared to be futile. Leonard Bloomfield (1933, p. 20), the principal figure

in the structural movement, remarked that any pronouncement on language universals would have to wait until more data could be amassed about particular languages. Bloomfield also found the speculative approach unacceptable for uncovering universals. For recent contributions to the theory of language universals, see Greenberg (1963) and Bach and Harms (1968).

5. Both Hockett (1958, p. 574) and Martinet (1964, p. 22) discuss that property of language whereby sounds and meanings operate in different patterns. Hockett calls it "duality of patterning" and Martinet, "double articulation."

6. A rule-by-rule remaking of grammar A into grammar B via a "transfer grammar" of the type envisioned by Harris would be an overly simplistic interpretation of foreign language learning. There are many extragrammatical factors to consider, among them, contextual clues and the motivation of the learner (see chapter 8). More importantly, the grammars of the native and target languages are built from both specific and universal elements. Aspect, for example, is easily recognizable as a grammatical category in Russian surface grammar while in English it is inextricably interwoven with tense. A rule-oriented approach to CA requires the recognition that some rules may have to be altered rather than added or dropped.

1.7 Background Readings

1. For general background reading in linguistics: Bolinger (1968); Langacker (1968); Lyons (1968); Dinneen (1967).

2. To acquire some skill in writing and understanding transformational grammar: Bach (1964); Koutsoudas (1966).

It is to be noted that neither the Bach book nor the one by Koutsoudas covers the latest developments in transformational theory. There is, however, no text of a more recent date that could be recommended to the beginning student. Word has it that both Bach and Koutsoudas are actively engaged in revising their books.

3. For a working knowledge of tagmemics, see Cook (1969).

4. A good survey of work being done in CA is Nemser (1970).

5. The reader may wish to consult Jakobovits (1970) in connection with the psychological implications of language learning.

6. For a recent discussion of the theory of CA and its application, see Moser (1970).

Chapter 2

THEORY AND PROCEDURES

2.1 Source and Goal (or Native and Target) Languages

In applying CA to language teaching, a distinction is often made between
the source (or native) language and goal (or target) language. Implied in the
use of these terms is a change of states, a movement away from the source or
native language toward the goal or target language, as the desired outcome of
the instructional program. Statements of contrast are made in terms of how
the source language interferes with the production of sentences in the goal
language or, alternatively, in terms of how the source language can be modified so that it provides for the production of sentences in the goal language.
If, for instance, we consider German as the target language and English as the
native language of a group of students, the rules of English which do not
correspond with those of German would have to be modified if the students
are to learn German. One of those rules deals with the ordering of verbal
elements in the predicate of declarative sentences. In German, the past parti-
cipial element is usually separated from the verbal auxiliary with the objective

noun phrase coming in between the two of them. Sentences like the following are produced:

Ich habe das Buch gelesen.

Its English counterpart does not have the past participle so separated:

I have read the book.

The modification of English grammar required to produce the German order of predication can be stated in the form of a transformation, as follows:

(English Predicate) AUX + PAST PART + OBJ NP ⟶
(German Predicate) AUX + OBJ NP + PAST PART

That is, the string of auxiliary (AUX), past participle (PAST PART), and objective noun phrase (OBJ NP) found in English predications is to be transformed to the string of auxiliary, objective noun phrase, and past participle in German. (This transformation is given only as an illustration of a kind of modification entailed in the use of "goal" and "source" in CA. Much greater elaboration would have to be made in order to contrast English sentences like *I had the book read by 6 o'clock* with their German counterparts.)

There are two other types of operation which would be necessary in terms of goal and source language: (1) Rules are added where the source language has none. With German as goal and English as source, it would be necessary to add rules to account for gender agreement of nouns and adjectives, e.g., *ein junger Mann,* 'a young man' *(junger,* masc. sing., in agreement with *Mann);* *ein kleines Kind,* 'a small child' *(kleines,* neuter sing., in agreement with *Kind).* (2) There is also deletion of rules where the source language makes grammatical distinctions not found in the goal language, e.g., the formation of tag questions, where English has specific rules for the choice of verb (*do, be, have, will,* etc.) and repetition of subject while German does not:

He has read the book, hasn't he?   Er hat das Buch gelesen, nicht wahr?
You have read the book, haven't you?   Du hast das Buch gelesen, nicht wahr?

Whatever the procedure involved in moving from source to goal (modification, addition, or deletion), the changes affect only the surface structures of the languages in question. Positing a common deep structure for languages is a necessity if we are to speak of a mutual convertibility from one particular language to another.

On the other hand the ideas of source (or native) and goal (or target) are not obligatory in performing a CA. Although it may be useful for the teacher to think of the grammar of one language as being acquired through a series of manipulations of the other language, no theoretical accommodation is made in such a view for the fact that the student does not necessarily forget the other language. The psychological processes undergone in the addition or rearrangement of grammatical rules are poorly understood. If, for example, formal instruction in a foreign language does not cause the student to forget his native language, it may very well lead him to forget elements of other foreign languages which he has studied. Moreover, persons who have learned a new language by living in a community where that language is spoken by a majority of the people often do forget certain parts of their native language. The reader would do well to keep in mind that "source" and "goal" (or native and target) have to do with application of CA and not with CA itself. (See the discussion on taxonomy and operation, below.)

2.2 Autonomous and Generalized Models

Depending on the linguist's theoretical orientation, the model he uses to organize his CA may be either autonomous or generalized. Autonomous models have no conscious correlation with a higher level of universals whereby overriding notions about language as the principal form of human communication are reinforced by each bit of specific information about particular languages. Generalized models, on the other hand, are constructed so that their application to particular languages reinforces the investigator's intuition about the universal structure of language. Just as the blueprint of a house leads to the building of a particular structure while, at the same time, sharing aspects with the structure of houses in general, so does each generalized model contain the elements of universal language structure.

Autonomous CAs have not been overly convincing to experts in the area of language instruction because the devices used to describe the language are not easily correlated to any psychological or pedagogical interpretation. The application of generalized models, while far from easily correlated with theories of language learning, at least provide universal tenets which, if supported psychologically, have far-reaching implications.

There are several linguistic models in use today which are capable of becoming generalized. Although the basic orientation of the present book is generative and transformational, it is altogether possible that other models, such as the tagmemic or stratificational ones, could also be generalized to accommodate linguistic universals. At the present time, however, only the generative and transformational model has been developed in this direction and, by the same token, is the most suitable to CA.

2.3 Taxonomy and Operation

A matter quite distinct from the question of autonomous and generalized models is the choice between a taxonomic and an operational study. While both may require a generalized base in order to be viable in CA, the methodology and the application can be quite different (although equally useful). To make a CA operational, contrasts would have to be expressed as a series of conversions performed on the source language in order to produce the forms of the goal language. (The examples given in the first section of this chapter could be considered operational.) Thus, the operational CA is a linguistic analog to those mental processes which may be at work in acquiring a foreign language. As such, its value depends upon how compatible it is to the psychological model of language learning which the teacher prefers. (In the discussion of "source" and "goal," some indication was given of the many psychological factors to be considered in adapting a CA to language instruction. No endorsement is given of a specific psychological theory of language learning.)

No goal of language acquisition is implied in a taxonomic CA. Instead, the analyst seeks those elements of grammar which are not shared by source and goal and identifies them according to their hierarchical importance. As an example, the operations given in section 1.1, converting the order of verbal elements in English predicates into that of German, could have been stated taxonomically under the heading of "unshared rules." It is important to understand that generalized models can be either taxonomic or operational in their format, but autonomous ones can be taxonomic only (see Table 2.1).

Table 2.1 Models of CA

Model	Taxonomic	Operational
Autonomous	x	
Generalized	x	x

Autonomous models lack the unifying force of a theory in which the particulars of each language are viewed as expressions of linguistic universals. Even though we might express a preference for generalized models which are also operational, we should realize that they are far more difficult to achieve than are taxonomic ones. First of all, there is no way of knowing for certain that the student will follow exactly the same set of conversion rules set down as part of the CA. Secondly, each rule of conversion must be formulated with extreme care so that it does not impinge incorrectly on any other rule. While taxonomic CAs should also be done so that all particulars mesh within the total framework, operational models put a greater demand on the compatibility of rules. Purely taxonomic statements can be far more effective, then, in handling contrasts which involve minutiae of structure. In obvious but detailed areas of contrast, operational models would also require that all entailed matters be treated as well.

In general linguistic theory, the concept "taxonomic" is often opposed to "generative." No such opposition is intended in this book. The taxonomy which gives form to our CA is based on the generative rules of the languages that are being contrasted. Robert Longacre (1968, p. 11) explains the value and use of a taxonomy in linguistics as follows:

> To what degree, then, is linguistics a taxonomic science? This is surely a question to which this generation of linguists should give considerable attention. But this question cannot even be entertained by those who have decided that taxonomy has no place in linguistics. Nevertheless, it seems obvious that the various units and relations of a language can be laid out, classified, and labelled in a manner not unlike the cataloguing of flora and fauna with labelled identification of their functioning parts.

2.4 Competence and Performance

In any study of language, it is important to distinguish between what a speaker says and what he is capable of saying. A speaker's language competence is his ability to produce and understand sentences in whatever language he may speak. If he is a speaker of English, he is able to recognize that the following sentences are somehow related:

1. John read the book.
2. What John did was to read the book.
3. It was John who read the book.
4. The book was read by John.

He is also able to understand that the same preposition can mark different functions, as in sentences like:

5. He was shot in the war.
6. He was shot in the leg.

He knows that the prepositional phrase in sentence 5 is an expression of time and can possibly be rephrased as *during the war*, while the prepositional phrase of sentence 6, although it begins with the same preposition, is locational and cannot be so rephrased. For as long as man has attempted to explain his language rationally, he has realized that each speaker has such abilities (although these abilities have not been formulated in precisely this way). We can think of written grammars as efforts to capture in a formal way the system in which these abilities operate.

There are many facets to the notion of competence. A person's ability to understand the sentences of a language may be greater than his ability to produce them. In foreign language study, such is often the case. Students appear to develop the ability to understand far more than they can say. It might be useful to differentiate these abilities by labeling the former one "receptive competence" and the latter "productive competence." Ambiguities such as the one in the sentence

    7. Flying planes can be dangerous.

may exist only for the listener, i.e., only with respect to receptive competence, since the person who uttered the sentence presumably knew which he meant: (a) that the flying of planes is dangerous or (b) that planes which fly are dangerous. Because no way has yet been devised to describe receptive and productive competence in terms of different grammars, we shall assume that they can be characterized in the same way, that is, with the same grammar.

A speaker's performance is an instance of his competence in action. Underlying each sentence that he utters is a system of grammar which he shares to a large extent with the hearer. It is also observable that the speaker's performance is affected by factors extraneous to his competence. Lack of interest, change of mind, distraction, and illness can cause stuttering, false starts, scrambling of word order, and even abrupt stops in the middle of sentences. Charles Hockett (1958, p. 143) gives the following example of a native speaker's performance in English:

> "It's uh . . . it's hu not . . . . I mean . . . [throat cleared] actually well he he we we had just sort of . . . in many ways sort of given up . . . trying to do very much . . . until . . . bedtime."

The hearer who has a competence in English can unscramble the sentence and edit out the extraneous parts. Hockett, himself, provides the following revision of it:

> "We had (in many ways) just sort of given up trying to do much until bedtime."

Of course there is no implication here that performance is always full of such phenomena. Some speakers perform (i.e., speak) more skillfully than others. Furthermore, there are times when each of us can speak with a modicum of false starts, scrambling, etc. Whatever the case may be, communication is achieved if the speaker's competence is similar to that of the hearer.

The relationship between language performance and competence is very much like that of the concert pianist who gives many performances, no two of which are exactly alike but each representing his musical abilities. Just as it is difficult to judge the range of a musician's knowledge of music by hearing one or a few of his performances, so it is difficult to know the structure of a speaker's competence by listening to a few sentences said by him. For this reason, the linguist who amasses a corpus of sentences of a language does it with the understanding that these sentences are only samples of what is possible in the language. The foreign language teacher, conversely, builds competence by using the sentences given as examples in the text to guide his students in producing novel but possible sentences of the language. Innovation is a demonstration of competence.

If we understand grammars as being formal explanations of competence, we can see that each grammar represents a model of speaker and hearer of the language it seeks to explain. Since the foreign language teacher is concerned with the building of new competences, it is appropriate that he contrast the grammar of the language being taught with that of his students. Criticism about the usefulness of CA in predicting learning errors (e.g., Wardhaugh 1970) does not seem to make a clear distinction between competence and performance. The teacher is well advised not to assume that every linguist's description of a language is, ipso facto, accurate and therefore a true portrayal of an ideal speaker's competence. Even if we could obtain accurate and complete descriptions of competences, comparing them would not lead to prediction of actual instances of error. To know exactly when a student will commit a given error would require a vast body of information about performance. While psychologists are beginning to amass data on memory retention, age and sex factors, and the limitations on embedding, much work remains to be done before any model of performance in language learning can emerge.

A systematic CA of two language competences, source and goal, provides the basis for *potential* error commission. Just how the teacher decides to handle such potential trouble spots depends on factors independent of interlanguage differences. It is only when much more is known about language performance that we will be able to decide which of several strategies is best applied in each instance. It is clear, in any event, that the CA of idealized competences (whether they are accurate or not) constitutes the very foundation of all applied studies in language teaching. In fact, to fully understand the subject matter of the present text, the reader must realize that all discussions of grammar are in terms of idealized competences. Performance factors are considered in the last chapter, with reference to language instruction.

2.5 Universal and Particular Grammar

The importance for CA of distinguishing between universal and particular grammar was touched upon in the first chapter. Briefly defined, universal grammar comprises all essential characteristics of human language. Particular grammar covers the unique ways in which each language interprets these essentials. Grouped under the heading of universal grammar would be (1) the general design of language; (2) certain elements, called "substantive" universals; and (3) some arrangements, called "formal" universals. We shall have more to say about language design in chapter 3, as well as about substantive and formal universals. Suffice it to say at this point that substantive universals can be thought of as units which result from man's need to name and describe the objects of his environment and their relationships to him and to one another. Formal universals are those constraints which man places on his language in order to avoid needless redundancies, ambiguities, and obstacles to efficient communication.

Linguists who have been concerned with language universals, notably Joseph Greenberg, have rejected the speculative methods of previous ages and have, instead, adopted logic in their research. For example, one of Greenberg's (1963) universals concerns the expression of number as distinct from singular or plural. (A remnant of dual number can be found in English in the use of *both* with two objects or persons, e.g., *both feet,* and *all* for more than two, e.g., *all of his teeth.*) Greenberg observed that, while the expression of dualities implies plurality beyond two, the converse is not true. That is, languages which make a distinction between *one* and *many* do not automatically distinguish between *two* and *many.* But languages with dual number also have plurality.

There are many other features of language which are good candidates for the title universal although they have not been investigated with the rigor of inductive logic. Among such features are (1) interrogation, (2) proposition formation, (3) identification of ego, and (4) denial and acceptance. We can make such speculations because we must consider language as a part of man's social structure. Thus, it is difficult to imagine a society of man where no one could ask questions, reason from cause and effect, tell others that he is sick or hungry, or never agree on a topic of discussion. Subsequent chapters deal with the various ways in which such needs are expressed in man's languages.

Suggestive of the existence of universals is the research on the acquisition of language by children. The naming of objects with or without some comment about them is a recurrent observation of children's speech at early stages. Children appear to learn how to diversify surface structures from simple pivotal and open-class words into more complex patterns. Eric Lenneberg (1967; pp. 145, 191-198, etc.) discusses some types of language disorder resulting from brain damage. Since the symptoms of aphasia, or the loss of speech, can apparently be observed among speakers of all languages, it seems likely that these symptoms are manifested in terms of universally shared features. Among the various forms that aphasia can take, there are two that have particular relevance to syntax: paraphasia and anomia. In one type of paraphasia, the patient produces ungrammatical sentences like the following (Lenneberg, p. 194):

"I haven't been headache troubled not for a long time. A kind of little ver [bird], machinery, a kind of animal do for making a sound."

In such cases, the ability to produce the correct arrangements of grammatical elements is lost.

The patient suffering anomia, on the other hand, has difficulty recalling the names of things. In his efforts to communicate, he may give lengthy descriptions about the thing, what its function is, or what associations it has with other things, without ever naming it.

The supposition that no two languages in the world are irreconcilable and thus that they share universal features directs us to look for the differences between them in their particular grammars. In other words, the directions of our study are shaped in predetermined ways—around proven and proposed universals. This is not to say, however, that variations among languages will not be great. From what we already know, variation is almost limitless. Limitless, but not fundamental.

2.6 Deep and Surface Structure

With reference to the universal design of language, some linguists (especially Chomsky 1965, Fillmore 1968) have proposed that all sentences have both a deep and a surface structure. The deep structure is an abstraction which contains all elements necessary for the production of semantically related surface sentences. For example, the sentences

1. The boy sees the girl.   2. The girl is seen by the boy.

derive from the same deep structure, although they are different on the surface. In each case, there is an agent (the boy), an objective (the girl), and an action (see). Following Fillmore (1968), the deep structure for both sentences can be described in terms of the tree diagram (Figure 2.1). The surface rules of English are such that, if the objective, *the girl,* is made the subject of the sentence (note that "subject" is a surface term), then its K is deleted, and the K of the agent is expressed as the preposition *by.*

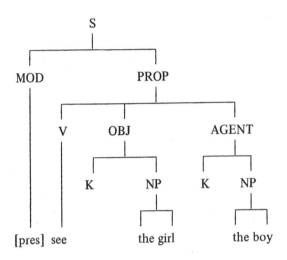

Figure 2.1   Diagram of "The boy sees the girl."

Deep structures, being unordered lineally, also require surface ordering rules such as: "Place objective subjects first in the sentence, followed by the verb, followed by the agentive, etc." The result of these rules would be the sentence:

The girl is seen by the boy.

The active counterpart to this sentence, namely, *The boy sees the girl,* is likewise derived via a set of realization rules, such as: "If agent is made subject of sentence, then delete K; objective becomes object of sentence, and its K is also deleted, etc." Applying other rules would yield related sentences such as

What the boy does is see the girl.
Seeing the girl is what the boy does.

and so on. As Fillmore points out, sentences with strikingly different surface structures may have similar deep structures and vice versa. The following sentences have similar surface structures but different deep structures:

Helen is easy to please.   Helen is eager to please.

or

Herman always dances with pretty girls.
Herman always dances with wild abandon.

Sometimes several deep structures yield identical surface sentences, such as:

The psychologists discussed courtship patterns among the chimpanzees.
The chief had the anthropologist for lunch.

When one surface structure has more than a single deep representation, it is said to be *ambiguous.*

For those readers who are acquainted with Noam Chomsky's 1957 position regarding the transformation of sentences, the interpretation of one deep structure underlying related but equally derived surface structures represents a significant departure from the earlier position on such matters. In the 1957 model, some sentences (defined as *kernels)* were thought to derive through obligatory transformations from the phrase structure while others *(nonkernel sentences)* had to be derived by optional transformations (see Chomsky 1957, p. 61). Thus the active sentence

The boy saw the girl.

was the result of obligatory transformations, while the passive sentence

The girl was seen by the boy.

resulted from the application of optional transformational rules. Now that both active and passive sentences (as well as other types) are considered similarly remote from an underlying structure, the labeling of transformations as either optional or obligatory no longer has any theoretical significance.

The implications of the concepts of deep and surface structures for CA are widespread. If there is indeed a deep structure underlying every sentence in a language, we can entertain the possibility that there is a deep structure which is shared by all languages. Furthermore, the peculiarities of particular grammar are to be found primarily in the kinds of deep-to-surface rules that each language has. It is not difficult to find illustrations of a deep and a surface structure in other languages. In French, for example, the sentences

Je suis intelligent.   Je suis Jean

have very much the same surface structure. The second, however, is related to another surface sentence:

Jean, c'est moi.

while it is ungrammatical in French to say

*Intelligent, c'est moi.

In Spanish, the sentence

Se lo dió a las tres.

can mean either 'He [or she] gave it to the three of them' or 'He [or she] gave it to him [or her or them] at three o'clock.' The Italian sentence

Nor mi piace il ritratto di Maria.

can mean either 'I don't like the picture [taken] of Maria' or 'I don't like the picture that belongs to Maria.'

If we apply the notions of deep and surface structure to the CA of two languages, it becomes clear that the most crucial area of contrast is the one between the deepest and the most surface structures. The following examples illustrate how the differences between languages must come at various levels of intermediate structure. Contrasting the structures that build

It is raining.　　[English]

and

Llueve.　　[Spanish]

we find that differences are found at no less than two distinct intermediate levels: (1) the generation of a subject form 'it' in English in accordance with a rule that English sentences of this type require a subject, while no comparable rule is found in Spanish, and (2) the modal system of English generates a progressive aspect which does not operate in the same way in Spanish.

Comparing

It is raining.　　[English]

with

Es regnet.　　[German]

we find that the difference in aspect still holds but that German, as well as English, generates a dummy subject *(es = it)* in such cases. Spanish, on the other hand, shares more intermediate rules with languages like Italian, as exemplified not only by expressions like Spanish *Llueve = Piove* in Italian but also by a variety of possible sentences. The poem *La gloria del momento* by Juseph Tusiani is bilingual; that is, it is written so that it can be taken as being either Spanish or Italian. (The orthography of Spanish requires the marking of certain accents, e.g., *poesía.)*

La gloria del momento

Con verde blando
viene cantando
la primavera:
viene cantando
al cielo al monte
al fresco mar radiante,
gloria celeste
musica agreste
rosa infinita:
sublime, santa,
viene la poesia,
la primavera canta.
  Delira, respira
  con brio
  sereno
  la lira
  del rio
  sublime, santa
  viene la poesia
  la primavera canta.

Since it is possible to show that the differences between languages can be found at any number of stages between the deep and the surface structures, we are also provided with a metric to measure the similarity between languages; languages are similar to each other in proportion to the number and hierarchical ordering of rules shared in the intermediate levels. Thus Spanish shares more intermediate rules with Italian than either does with English or German. The four languages all share more of such rules than any of them does with Swahili. Finally, Spanish, Italian, English, German, *and* Swahili *all* share the deepest level of structure because they are all human languages and are all equally accessible to human learners. At this deepest level would be all of the most basic elements of human language, such as SENTENCE, MODALITY, and PROPOSITION. (See chapter 4 for the discussion of deep structure.)

2.7 Concerning Realism in the Writing of Grammar

The following question might well be asked with regard to the claims made about hierarchical ordering, deep and surface structure, and universals in language: In what ways are such linguistic constructs related to models of perception and neurological activity in the brain? In other words, what psychological and/or physiological reality do the linguist's grammars have? To date, there is no conclusive evidence that any of the linguist's rules are analogous to the mental processes the speaker goes through in forming his sentences.

We might, however, speculate that at least some of our grammatical pronouncements have psychological correlates. Hierarchical ordering is one case in point. The expression of number by a speaker of English, for example, might be considered as relevant to a more basic level in the hierarchy than his control of the particulars of noun pluralization. Therefore, the rule that permits the pluralization of *boy* and *man* is more basic than the ones that stipulate that the plural of *boy* is *boys* but that of *man* is *men*. In searching for psychological correlates, then, we should be concerned first with the general notion of number and secondly with its particular expressions. Yet, we should not be overly concerned, at this point, that our rules always match some psychological data. Chomsky (1968, p. 12) has the following to say about the matter:

> It seems to me that the most hopeful approach today is to describe the phenomena of language and of mental activity as accurately as possible, to try to develop an abstract theoretical apparatus that will as far as possible account for these phenomena and reveal the principles of their organization and functioning, without attempting, for the present, to relate the postulated mental structures and processes to any physiological mechanisms or to interpret mental function in terms of "physical causes".

As of now, deep and surface structures, with their intermediate levels, and language universals are extremely useful in CA. Whatever support exists for their psychological and physiological "validity" is indeed welcome, but not essential.

2.8 Procedures for CA

The ways in which we contrast two languages are motivated by several theoretical considerations. First of all, our model must be generalized. That is to say, it must proceed in terms of forms and functions which are presumed to be universal. Whatever we say about either language involved in the contrastive procedure must be reconcilable to a general theory of how human language is designed. We shall also require that our model of contrast have a leveled structure, going from a deepest level through various intermediate levels to a surface level. Differences are found in the intermediate levels of structuring and increase as the surface structure is approached. Whatever contrasts are found, they are to be considered strictly in terms of linguistic competence and not in terms of linguistic performance.

If the results of the CA are to be applied to error prediction in language learning, factors of performance must be incorporated. The strategy used to develop competence in the areas of contrast may also play a significant role in error prediction. Sequencing of instructional material may be conducive to certain kinds of error by the student. In other words, the strategy of instruction cannot be assumed to be isomorphic with the statement of contrasts. Areas of contrast can be covered in many ways, and these ways must be evaluated as to their efficacy in promoting good performance (see chapter 8 for further discussion).

Finally, the results of our CA may be presented either taxonomically or operationally. Although the conversion rules of an operational approach are more suggestive of the learning situation, there are many applications for which a taxonomy of contrasts is quite adequate. In either case, the grammatical theory which will be adopted in this book is the transformational-generative one. We chose this theory of language because it has proven to be the most explicit one available in regard to the treatment of universals, deep and surface structure, and the generative capacity of language. (See chapter 3 for additional discussion of grammar.)

The following steps are only suggestive of those to be followed in contrasting two languages:

1. The first step is to observe the differences between the surface structures of two languages. Such differences may range from total absence of some surface feature in one of the two languages to partial sharing of a feature. Thus, if we contrast Chinese with English, we will find in Chinese no overt number inflection to equate with that of English. Contrasting English with another language, say, Arabic, we would find quite a different situation with respect to number. Both languages turn out to have number inflection, but Arabic will be found to have a far more detailed surface treatment of it than English does. However great the contrasts, we assume, in this first step, that they are explainable in terms of some underlying universal.

2. The second step is to postulate the underlying universals. To continue with the example given in step 1, we postulate that the universal in question is NUMBER (universals are written in caps). In doing so, we provide ourselves with the necessary reference frame to discuss even those situations where

NUMBER is not overtly realized. (We observe also that speakers of Chinese are able to express number distinctions by adding any of a set of specific numbers to nouns, producing the equivalent of *one book, two book, three book,* and so on.)

3. The third step is to formulate the deep-to-surface (realizational) rules concerning the various expressions of NUMBER in each of the languages involved in our CA. We do *not,* however, produce two complete and separate sets of realizational rules. Since our interests are contrastive, nothing useful would be gained by such a step. Instead, we specify *only those rules which are not shared.* In this way, at least one of the contrasts in number realization between Chinese and English is statable in a rule of the following form:

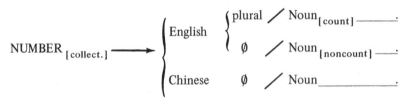

That is to say, where NUMBER is collective, English nouns will be pluralized if they are countables. If they are noncountables, they will not be pluralized. The following sentences illustrate countable and noncountable nouns that are used collectively:

Countable: John bought books, pencils, and rulers.

Noncountable: Helen bought paper, glue, and ink.

As for Chinese, the rule simply states that no pluralization is made ($\emptyset$).

In this third step, we may decide to make our CA operational (section 2.3). In doing so, we label one of the languages as the goal (or target) language and the other as the source (native) language. For example, we can make Chinese the goal and require that the English part of the rule for NUMBER specification be converted into the Chinese part:

English plural ⟶ Chinese $\emptyset$ Noun $_{[count, noncount]}$ ——:
(source)   (goal)

If, on the other hand, we make Chinese the source language, our conversion procedure is essentially one of adding two English rules:

a. Noun $\longrightarrow$ $\begin{cases} \text{Noun}_{[\text{count}]} \\ \\ \text{Noun}_{[\text{noncount}]} \end{cases}$

b. NUMBER $\longrightarrow$ $\underset{[\text{collect.}]}{}$ $\begin{cases} \text{plural} \quad / \ \text{Noun}_{[\text{count}]} \underline{\qquad}. \\ \\ \emptyset \quad / \ \text{Noun}_{[\text{noncount}]} \underline{\qquad}. \end{cases}$

Rule *a* differentiates nouns into the two classes of countables and noncountables, and rule *b* is a recapitulation of the English part of the combined realizational rule given above.

There is no implication in these contrasts that the English-speaking student of Chinese will find it easier to learn the different rules for NUMBER realization than will the Chinese-speaking student of English. Whether it is easier to forget surface rules than it is to learn them remains a matter to be validated by carefully controlled psychological experimentation. In any event, there is no requirement to make the CA operational. The rule of NUMBER specification, as first formulated above, in which both English and Chinese realizations are presented, conveys the essentials of the contrast in a completely adequate way.

2.9 Topics for Discussion

1. Taking any existent CA—such as the ones involving German, Spanish, and Italian: Kufner (1962), Moulton (1962), Agard and Di Pietro (1965, 1965a), Stockwell and Bowen (1965), Stockwell, Bowen, and Martin (1965)—discuss the ways in which linguistic universals are treated either explicitly or implicitly. Are the models employed in these CAs best characterized as generalized or as autonomous? What evidence is there that contrasts have been stated taxonomically or operationally?

2. Which of the following could be proposed as linguistic universals: (a) pronominalization as a process or pronouns as a category; (b) the use of reflexives; (c) nasalized vowels; (d) definitizing as a process or the definite article as a category. Give reasons for your opinions.

3. Discuss ways in which the contrasting of languages might also shed light on the universals of language.

4. Suggest factors affecting language performance in addition to the ones mentioned in this chapter.

5. It has been proposed that the following sentences in English derive from the same deep structure:

a. I like to read.
b. Reading is what I like to do.
c. What I like to do is read.

Contrast them with comparable sentences in another language. How does the contrast bear out a claim that the deep structures of such sentences would be universal?

6. What evidence is obtainable from CA that the so-called dummy subject of sentences in English like the following is not to be found in the deep structure?

a. It is cold.
b. It is five o'clock.

2.10 Notes

1. Rosen (1969, p. 20) points out that a requirement for a hierarchical theory is that the level lying lowest (i.e., the most basic) in the order be universal. Otherwise it would be impossible to make certain that all information about higher level elements is unambiguous. Although Rosen's remarks are made in the context of automata theory, the implications for our deep-surface distinction are obvious. If it should turn out that a feature of our postulated deep level does not lead unambiguously to an explanation of how that feature is realized in the surface structure of the languages involved in CA, our only alternative is to revise our interpretation of the deep structure.

2. Ideally, at least two alternative solutions are necessary to evaluate the output of a CA. Each can be judged in terms of how well they meet the four requirements of completeness, accuracy, explicitness, and simplicity. It is inevitable that one solution will emerge formally superior. In the application of the CA to classroom instruction, however, the evaluation procedure is complicated by factors such as the sequence of presentation and the type of drills used by the teacher. It is impossible to determine either the accuracy or the instructional effectiveness of a CA in language teaching unless careful consideration is made of the particular pedagogical approach used. (See chapter 8 for discussion of details.)

3. Although CA is addressed to uncovering linguistic diversity, the process cannot be meaningful unless it rests on a foundation of supposed similarities

in language structure. An endeavor conversely related to CA is linguistic typ-ology, which seeks to classify languages in terms of how they share similar features of structure. Both CA and linguistic typology can be based on the same theoretical foundations. The only differences are to be found in their goals. For an indication of how the notions of deep and surface structure can be applied to a typology, see Fillmore (1968, p. 51 ff.)

4. Linguistic models have been frequently applied to the study of bilingual-ism. Jakobovits (1970, p. 169 ff.) gives a survey of how various psycholo-gists have attempted to characterize bilingual speech as the interplay between separately defined language competences (specified as Language *A* and Lan-guage *B)*. Whatever is hypothesized about language structure by the linguist is open to implementation in psychological research.

2.11 Background Readings

1. For autonomous models of CA: Lado (1957).

2. On competence and performance:
      General theory: Hockett (1958); Chomsky (1965).
      Applications to FL teaching: Di Pietro (1970).

3. On universal and particular grammar:
      Greenberg (1963); Bach and Harms (1968).

4. On deep and surface structure:
      Theory: Fillmore (1968).
      Applications: Goldin (1968), applying Fillmore's model; Jacobs and Rosenbaum (1968) contains exercises in the separation of deep and surface structure but does not follow Fillmore's approach; Kessler (1969) with refer-ence to CA of English and Italian; Rutherford (1968) in the context of Eng-lish as a foreign language.

Chapter 3

MULTIDIMENSIONAL ASPECTS

OF LANGUAGE DESIGN

To a certain extent, the language teacher must be his own grammarian. He must arrive at some conceptualization of how language is organized in general if he is to prepare teaching materials which systematically cover all matters of importance to his students. No matter what his approach to teaching may be (he may decide never to openly formulate rules of grammar), he must proceed according to some master blueprint of grammar. At the very least, he must understand the grammatical plan adopted by the writer of his textbook. As Dwight Bolinger has pointed out (1968, pp. 38 ff.), foreign language textbooks are traditionally constructed according to a tripartite view of language. Such texts usually contain exercises and drills treating pronunciation, word formation, and syntax. To be aware that textbooks have a grammatical plan is an important beginning—but just that. To function efficiently, the teacher needs to develop a technique for evaluating the grammatical coverage with respect to its extent and its accuracy. If he has a view of language design in which several interpretations of grammatical organization have been synthesized, he will be able to go beyond the grammatical plan of the textbook toward more comprehensive coverage of his own making. In the present chapter, we shall review three major views of language design and then present a plan which is more comprehensive than any of them.

Syntax
Morphology
Phonology

Figure 3.1 Levels of structure

The structural school of linguistics held more or less to the notion that language design was tripartite. Structuralists looked upon these parts as levels and labeled them phonology, morphology, and syntax (Figure 3.1). This basic design was elaborated in various ways. Kenneth Pike, for example, interpreted each level in terms of three different manifestations: as units, as arrangements of units, and as a system which schematizes the relationships of units (Pike 1959). In phonology, for example, the units are phonemes; the arrangements are the various combinations of phonemes in syllables and parts of syllables (diphthongs, consonant clusters, etc.); and, finally, the system of relationships can be illustrated by vowel diagrams and charts of consonants.

With the development of transformational-generative theories, language design came to be differentiated into so-called components. Central importance was given to syntax (called the base component) while phonology, together with what was previously termed morphology, acquired the role of an interpretive component. Semantics, hitherto outside the scope of formal linguistic study, was incorporated into the general design and also given an interpretive role (Figure 3.2). In this view, syntactic relationships comprise the fundamentals of language. These syntactic relationships (stated in the form of rules) are vested with meaning (through the semantic component) and with sound (through phonology). It should be pointed out that not all

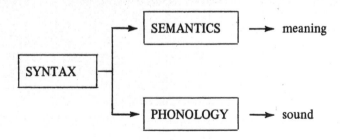

Figure 3.2 Componential view

transformationalists accept the position that syntax is the base component. In fact, some linguists hesitate to separate syntax from semantics in any significant way. Others would not even entertain the possibility that language can be broken up into components. This last group tends to think of language as one inseparable set of rules, starting with the most general aspects and ending with the most detailed. Yet, even in this last view, it is convenient to think of rules as operating in certain areas which can roughly be defined as syntactic, semantic, and phonological. The componential view of language design is still a very practical one.

The deep-to-surface dimension which has been proposed (chapter 2) would intersect, in some ways, the components of language. Semantics and a part of syntax are seen as deep structure, and the remainder of syntax and all of phonology are on the surface of language. The major reason for proposing such a dimension is that some linguists feel a necessity to distinguish between a level of grammar where formal relationships are invariable and one where variation occurs. Terms like "subject" and "predicate" are relevant to surface structure while "agent" and "objective" function in deep structure. Among the different interpretations of deep structure which linguists have made, Fillmore's strikes us as being the most adaptable to CA. (The specifics of deep and surface structure are treated in chapters 4 and 7.)

To incorporate each of the views presented above into one master scheme of language design would be difficult, if not altogether impossible. Yet each of them has captured some general property of language which bears on the contrasting of particular languages and is therefore of use to the language teacher. As a result, our design of language is multidimensional:

1. It has separate components, labeled semantics, syntax, and phonology.

2. It has levels of structure, starting with a deep level and progressing to a surface level through a series of intermediate rules.

3. It is generative, that is, statable in terms of rules which are predictive of all sentences possible in a language and not restricted to a single corpus of them.

In Figure 3.3, a presentation is made of our general view of language design. It is, of course, difficult to represent the fact that it is generative. In the following discussion, the design will be elaborated and a more detailed diagram of it provided (Figure 3.4).

Box 1 in Figure 3.3 contains those rules which combine semantic features with syntactic rules, and in box 2 are the rules converting syntactic and semantic elements into sound. Because of the complexity of language, even a multidimensional design leaves much unsaid. The reader should keep in mind

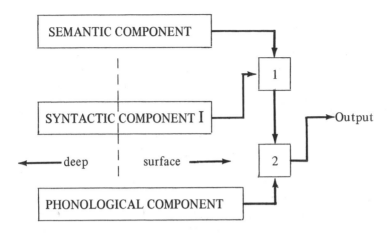

Figure 3.3   General view of language design

that further refinement or even refutation of parts of the model may come in the future as a result of our knowing more about language.

3.1 The Components

The interpretation of language as having separate phonological, syntactic, and semantic components reflects the major divisions of contemporary linguistic research far more accurately than the previous structural approach, which excluded semantics and distinguished between phonology and morphology. Because its physical properties (sounds) are accessible to study by instruments, the phonological component is the most thoroughly researched of the three.

It is not necessary to think of language as primarily consisting of syntactic structures. The componential view of language design can be accepted without the requirement that syntax be more basic than either phonology or semantics. While our diagram shows syntax in the middle position between semantics and phonology, the order could have been easily changed so that semantics would occupy the middle. (Note that syntax and semantics are tied together through a set of rules, box 1, before both are aligned with phonology through the rules of box 2.) Certainly, the ways in which transformations relate sentences in a language cannot be discussed without reference to the semantic elements which are involved in those transformations. Rather than assert that it is the syntactic arrangement that invokes specific semantic "fillers" (or even, for that matter, that syntactic arrangements are motivated by semantics), we refrain from going beyond the observation that syntax and semantics are intimately connected and that neither is profitably discussed without reference to the other. As we shall see later on, each language selects not only the semantic features it considers useful but also the syntactic arrangements in which those features are found. Arabic, for example, restricts passive sentences from expressing agent while English does not, although C. C. Fries noted some time ago that passive sentences in English more frequently exclude the agent than include it. We shall also require that syntactic primes be as devoid of referential meaning as possible. Thus NAME, CASE, etc., are syntactic primes which provide general categories to be filled by semantic elements. In this way, the specifics of CASE (agent, instrument, etc.) are considered as elements of semantics rather than of syntax. This interpretation is in opposition to that of Fillmore (1968), who treats the specifics of CASE as syntactic. The difference in interpretation need not affect the stating of rules, but rather labels as semantic a part of what has been called syntactic.

Of the three components, progress in semantics moves at the slowest pace. Many problems remain to be solved in the establishment of unquestionable norms for discovery and in disentangling the linguist's use of semantics from that of the philosopher or the logician. It may well be that contrasting the semantic fields of different languages will prove to be the best way to approach the treatment of semantic features. Attempts to restrict semantic analysis to one language are questionable and open to attack. See, for example, Bolinger's criticism (1965) of Katz and Fodor's (1963) treatment of the English word *bachelor*. More will be said about the establishment of semantic features in chapters 5 and 6.

The phonological component is understood to comprise all features and processes having to do with the realization of syntactic and semantic elements as sound (see Chomsky and Halle 1968, p. 7; Harms 1968, p. 1). A recent and major departure from the view of phonology as developed by the structural linguists is the deemphasis on phonemic units. The autonomous interpretation of phonemes as basic phonological units not only made it difficult to talk about patterns of specific features, such as the voicelessness of stops which follow [s] in initial clusters in English—[sp], [st], [sk]—but also required the association of phonetic features to syntax and semantics to be considered under the heading of morphophonemics. Although some structural linguists, notably Hockett (1958), carefully avoided labeling morphophonemics as a separate level of language, the temptation to do so was not resisted by others. (For further discussion, see Hockett 1961.) In place of autonomous phonemes, some transformationalists talk about systematic phonemes, but even these are given little importance. Robert T. Harms (1968, p. 1) explains the view on phonemes as follows:

> The phoneme—specifically, the systematic phoneme—has a clearly sec-
> ondary status, but, for matters of presentation, it is frequently convenient
> to refer to phonemes as the underlying segments used to designate or
> "spell" morphemes—i.e., segments containing the minimum number of
> distinctive feature-specifications required to account for the phonetic re-
> alization of morphemes.

It is this view of the systematic phoneme which we shall adopt in our discussions of phonology, the main purpose of which is to characterize semantic
and syntactic elements as strings of sound.

We shall now proceed to outline the specifics of each component. Keep in
mind, however, that the organization presented herein is not universally accepted by theorists. Indeed, arguments rage over practically every specific
(see, for example, McCawley 1968). Semantics, especially, is open to debate.
Our only claim is that the design allows for the identification and explanation
of contrasts between languages. While those contrasts which we discuss appear to be fundamental ones, there is no guarantee that revisions of the design
will not allow for the expression of even more basic contrasts. The design
is the result of putting together elements discussed by several theorists, e.g.,
Katz and Fodor (1963), Chomsky and Halle (1968), Fillmore (1968), and
Bach (1964).

3.2 The Syntactic Component

We keep in mind that the traditional interpretation of syntax is that it is
that part of grammar which deals with arrangements. Thus the basic elements
of the syntactic component as presented here are units expressing arrangement and the arrangements themselves. Thus NAME is a unit of arrangement
which refers to that property of human languages whereby objects and notions are indexed. VERBOID is the label given to another unit of arrangement which has to do with description of relationships among NAMES.

Arrangements are understood in two dimensions: (1) In the hierarchical
dimension, units are shown to be dominated by higher ranking units or to
be specifications of them. Thus

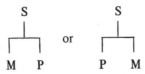

indicates that the units M(ODALITY) and P(ROPOSITION) are dominated by S(ENTENCE). (2) In the linear dimension, units are restricted as to the order in which they occur with respect to each other. Thus

may indicate that M precedes P and not vice versa. At the deepest level of syntax, units are not restricted linearly, only hierarchically. The linear restriction of units is specified in the specific grammar of each language.

At its deepest level, the syntactic component has a set of universal units, called *syntactic primes,* which are accompanied by a set of *syntactic ordering rules,* some of which are universal and some restricted to particular languages. The syntactic primes include NAME, SENTENCE, VERBOID, MODALITY, etc. The syntactic ordering rules cover the ways in which syntactic primes are put together, e.g., SENTENCE consists of MODALITY and PROPOSITION; PROPOSITION consists of VERBOID and any number of CASE CATEGORIES. The syntactic ordering rules tend to become more detailed as primes are specified. Involved in the surface realization of syntax are those rules which incorporate relevant semantic elements. These rules have been termed *semantic projection rules.* Other rules relate syntactic and semantic elements to features of sound. These are called *phonetic characterization rules.* (See Figure 3.4 for illustration of the syntactic and other components of language.)

3.3 The Semantic Component

Despite the criticism of some (cf. McCawley 1968) regarding the formal discussion of semantics in linguistic terms, we shall proceed to interpret the semantic component as comprising those discrete units of meaning whereby man characterizes elements of his life, his environment, his social structure, and his occupations. We find it useful to postulate features such as "animate," "inanimate," "vegetable," "male," "female," etc., to which we can assign plus or minus coefficients in the description of semantic structure and its impact on syntax. Just as we reject the autonomous phoneme as an essential unit, so do we reject the notion of "word" as basic to semantics. Each word is a composite of a number of semantic features (sometimes called "markers," as in Fodor and Katz 1964), just as phonemes are composites of features. For this reason, a discussion of the lexicon of a language (i.e., a collection of its words) must be considered one surface realization of the semantic features.

Operating on the stock of semantic features is a set of universal selection rules which produces redundant and universal matrices of features. It is from such matrices that language-specific matrices of features are formed by means of a secondary set of selection rules. To give some simple examples, Italian *dito* and English *finger* and *toe* all draw their semantic features from the same matrix of universals. If we provisorily label them [digital], [foot-attached], [hand-attached], etc., we can posit such features as deriving from a universal stock and associated to each other by a set of universal selection rules. The secondary set of selection rules then assigns plus or minus coefficients to each feature as it is found in each language. Thus *dito, finger,* and *toe* are all [+ digital], but *dito* is unspecified for [foot-attached] and [hand-attached] (Table 3.1). This is not to imply, of course, that the specification of *dito, finger,* and *toe* involve only these features. The matrix has been simplified to serve as an illustration of the procedure.

Table 3.1   Feature specification of dito, finger, and toe

Label	*dito*	*finger*	*toe*
Digital	+	+	+
Hand-attached	0	+	–
Foot-attached	0	–	+

The next step is to apply redundancy rules which show how the specification of some features in the matrix implies the others. Since [+ digital] in Italian implies either [+ hand-attached] or [+ foot-attached], we need discuss the semantics of *dito* by referring to [+ digital] alone. To explain the association of the other features, we write a redundancy rule of the type

$$[\text{+ digital}] \longrightarrow \begin{cases} [\text{+ hand-attached}] \\ [\text{+ foot-attached}] \end{cases}$$

This rule is to be read as follows: To the feature [+ digital] add either [+ hand-attached] or [+ foot-attached].

After redundancies have been accounted for, semantic features are associated with syntactic arrangements via a set of *projection rules*. In discussing projection of semantic features, it is important to understand that some features have a more pervasive effect on syntax than others have. In the case of

[+ digital] given above, we have a simple case of projection into a word class: *dito,* which is a noun in Italian. Other semantic features, such as [+ definite], may give rise to entire grammatical classes, such as the definite article,

$$N_{[def]} \rightarrow DET + N$$

As we shall see in chapter 5 (semantic projection), some semantic features figure strongly in establishing grammatical categories, while others are restricted to word classes. To give a simple example, if we were contrasting Russian with Italian or English, we would find that the projection of [+ definite] does not give rise in Russian to a grammatical element "definite article." Russian finds other ways to handle this semantic feature.

Semantic features play an important role in agreement and concord. Thus pronouns are aligned with specific antecedants according to such elements as [+ male], [+ animate], etc., in many languages of the world. A kind of concord that is not so obvious is the one involved in the selection of adjectives as modifiers of nouns. McCawley's example (1968) of

My buxom neighbor is the father of two.

is nongrammatical in English because the expression "buxom neighbor" does not stand in concord with "father of two." While "neighbor" can be either [+ male, − female] or [− male, + female], "buxom" can be only [− male, + female].

3.4 The phonological Component

Our interpretation of the design of the phonological component follows closely that of the semantic one. The prime difference is that much more research has been done on phonology, and the structure we propose here is more likely to go unquestioned. For example, we posit a universal stock of phonetic features which, although not exhaustively researched, is plausible because we can measure the flexibility of those parts of the human anatomy involved in speech. Furthermore, since man is anatomically endowed in equal ways, no human language has speech sounds which are unpronounceable by speakers of other languages. That is to say, there are no human speech sounds which require an extra set of teeth or the vibration of only one vocal chord—matters apparently outside the physical ability of man. (See Lieberman's experimentation at the University of Connecticut concerning the vocal tract of the chimpanzee.) Among the universal stock of phonetic features, we would include [voicing], [vocalicity], [aspiration], etc. These features are acted upon by a set of universal selection rules which produce redundant and universal matrices of sound features. In this way, some features become associated as more significant than others. The most significant ones are the major class features (Chomsky and Halle 1968, p. 299): [sonorant], [consonantal], and [vocalic], which serve to subclassify other features.

Through a set of secondary phonetic selection rules, language-specific matrices are established. Also assigned are the proper plus or minus coefficients for each feature. A perusal of any number of feature analyses of various languages (see, for example, Harms 1968) will show that each language groups and evaluates features in specific ways. Tenseness or laxness may figure strongly in one language and very little in another. Voicing, for example, is less important in the characterization of Mandarin stops than is aspiration.

It is to be kept in mind that the phonetic features referred to in this book are purely classificatory. The assignment of a plus coefficient (+) to the feature [aspiration] means that aspiration is distinctive in characterizing the sound segment under analysis. There may be many degrees of actual aspiration present in the production of sounds. Our intention, however, is to indicate only when it is *distinctively* present, that is, when it serves to differentiate aspirated from unaspirated sounds. The same may be said about any feature used to classify the sounds in a language. See Chomsky and Halle (1968, p. 297) for a clear presentation of this point.

Paralleling the redundancy rules of the semantic component is a set of *phonological redundancy rules* which operate on the specific phonetic matrix of the language. If it is found, for example, that [+ aspiration] always accompanies [– voiced] in the formation of occlusives ([– continuant]) such as [p t k] in a language but [– voiced] is present independently of [+ aspiration] in the description of other consonants in that language, [+ aspiration] is considered to be redundant with regard to [– voiced]. This redundancy is explainable via a rule of the type

$$[- \text{voiced}] \rightarrow [+ \text{aspiration}] \ / \ [\overline{-\text{continuant}}]$$

In Persian, for example, [p t k] are always aspirated while [f s] are not. The nonredundant description of both sets would not include the specification of aspiration:

$$[\text{p t k}]: \begin{bmatrix} -\text{ voiced} \\ -\text{ continuant} \\ \text{etc.} \end{bmatrix} \qquad [\text{f s}]: \begin{bmatrix} -\text{ voiced} \\ +\text{ continuant} \\ \text{etc.} \end{bmatrix}$$

The syntactic and semantic content of a language is characterized as complexes of sounds through a set of rules of the following type:

$$\text{PLU} \longrightarrow \begin{cases} \text{[s]} \; / \; \text{V} \# \underline{\hspace{1cm}} \# \\[2ex] \text{[es]} \; / \; \text{C} \# \underline{\hspace{1cm}} \# \end{cases}$$

That is to say, plural (PLU) is represented as [s] after words ending in a vowel (V#) and as [es] after words ending in a consonant (C#). (Note that we use "s" and "es" to stand for complexes of sound features wherever it is mnemonically useful. Otherwise, each feature or set of features is specified as needed.) Such a rule is applied in Spanish to produce

>   *casas*   from *casa* 'house' + PLU

and

>   *señores*   from *señor* 'Mr.' + PLU

Rules of this type are called *phonetic characterization rules.* Just as their semantic counterparts, the semantic projection rules, insert semantic features at different stages into the syntactic component, so do the phonetic characterization rules affect the semantic and syntactic composite of an utterance at different levels. Thus the rule that specifies permissible word shapes in a language is of a higher level than the rules that juxtapose morphemic entities, such as pluralization. In Spanish, for example, words ending in consonant plus [s] are not allowed. The pluralization rule explains exactly what happens when a morpheme characterized as a consonant is added to another morpheme with a consonant as its termination (señor).

Because phonetic characterization rules are ranged from general (high level to specific (low level), various patterns of sound to semantic or syntactic relationships are discerned in a language. It is the observation of such patterns that leads to the formalization of the grammar of a particular language. Observing that tense, person, mood, for example, are characterized in association with verbs in Spanish and yield certain patterns (called paradigms) makes it seem worthwhile to speak of verbal inflection in that language. The common association of gender in that language with word-final vowels *o* and *a* (*niño, niña,* etc.) figures importantly in the classification of nouns by Spanish grammarians as being either masculine or feminine. It is important to keep in mind the limitations of this view of grammar when we contrast languages.

We must distinguish clearly between the universal nature of tense, person, mood, gender, etc., and the particular association of them to the patterns of sounds in a language. (Note that the lack of a pervasive pattern of semantic or syntactic phonological association of such elements has led some investigators to speak of a language as not having that grammatical category; cf. the many discussions of gender in English.) It is easy to see, for example, that, while vowel terminations in Spanish correlate roughly with universal semantic features defined as [± male, ± female], the vowel terminations of many nouns serve simply to classify them according to the constraints of surface grammar in Spanish.

Just because other languages, such as English, do not show such patterns of semantic and phonological associations, one should not assume that it is impossible to speak of gender in those languages. Reflexes of universal gender may appear in other ways, such as in the cross-reference of pronouns to nouns (*the man—he, the woman—she,* etc.)

There is much more to be said about the specific structure of each component of the design of language. Further discussion will be found in subsequent chapters. What we have already said about the design can be illustrated as shown in Figure 3.4.

The design of language presented herein provides in some way for the general aspects discussed above. The primes of each component, together with their universal selection and ordering rules, represent what is shared by all languages. It is further proposed that languages begin to differentiate with the secondary set of selection and ordering rules. All rules, starting with the secondary ones of selection and ordering, are realizational insofar as they yield the surface structures of each language; some of these rules will turn out to be universal because of the requirement that expression of duality bring with it expression of plurality; cf. Greenberg (1963).

Rules of semantic projection and phonetic characterization are intercomponential, i.e., they serve to tie semantics and phonology to syntax. Following Chomsky (1965) et al., one could say that such rules furnish the link between *central* syntax and *interpretive* semantics and phonology.

Only the syntactic component is represented as having a deep-to-surface dimension, but, depending on one's position, it would not seem farfetched to recognize a surface-to-deep dimension in each of the three components. In this case, depth is equatable to the hierarchy in which we order our rules. In the view of many transformational linguists, of course, semantics is thought of as all deep and phonology as all surface. To depict such an interpretation in our diagram, we would have to extend diagonally the dotted line represent-

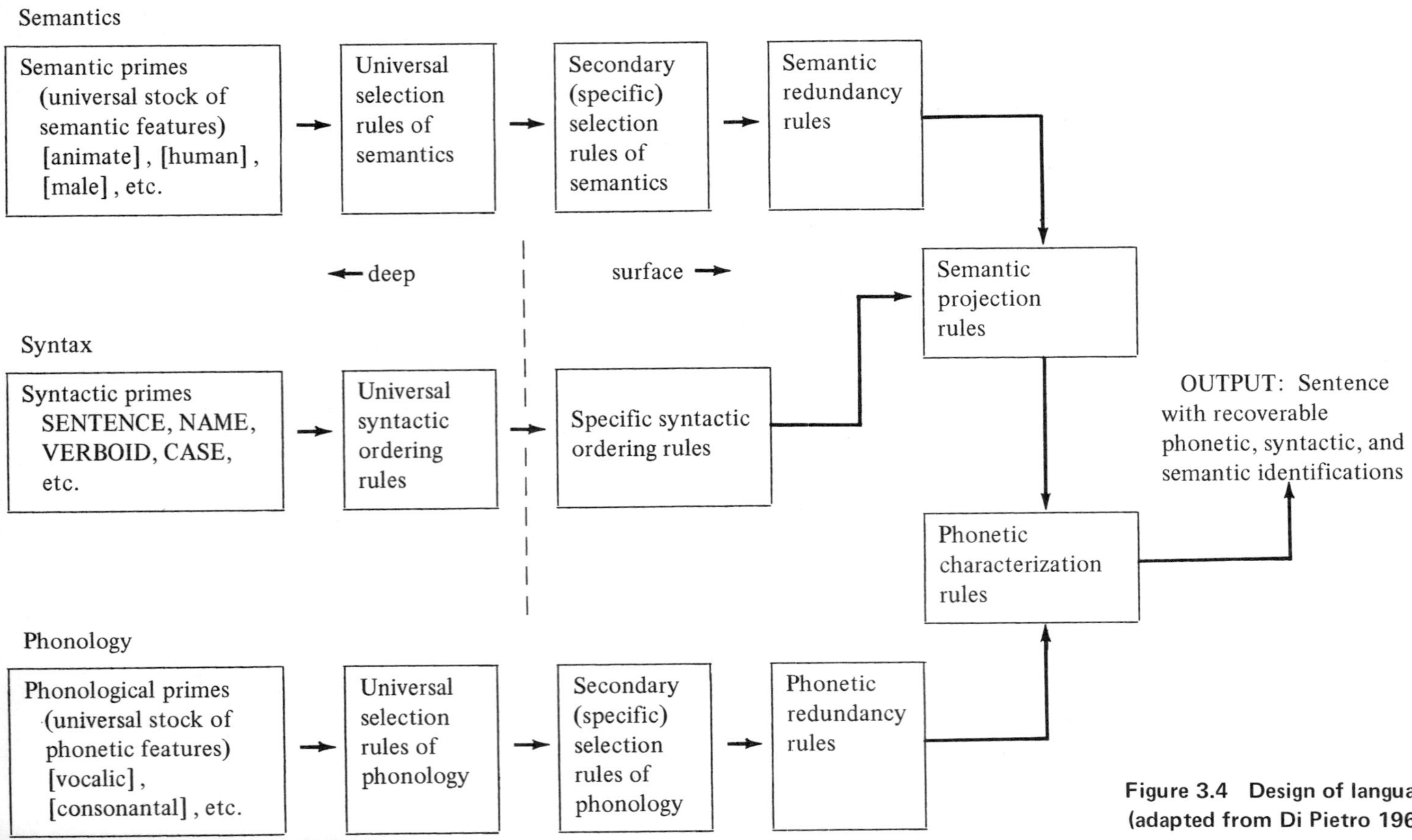

Figure 3.4 Design of language (adapted from Di Pietro 1968)

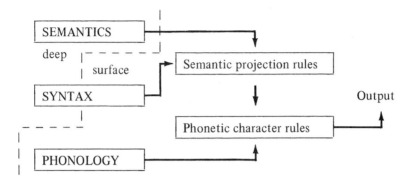

Figure 3.5 Alternative view of depth in language design

ing the deep and surface dichotomy so that all of semantics with the possible exception of the projection rules is deep and all of phonology is surface (Figure 3.5).

3.5 The Place of Style

Style is treated in this book as the set of choices each speaker makes in employing the rules made available to him by the language he is speaking. The set is determined not only by the speaker's personal preferences but also by the situation in which he wishes to communicate. Situations may range from formal to informal, from colloquial to official, etc. (see Martin Joos 1962).

The definition of style as the choice of rules available in a language under different circumstances and by different speakers makes it possible for us to explain how two languages may have a similar rule but invoke it under different circumstances. The active-passive set of transformations, for example, is found in both English and French:

English:	John drank the wine.	French:	Jean a bu le vin.
	The wine was drunk		Le vin a été bu
	by John.		par Jean.

When the agent is unexpressed in English, the choice seems to be for the passive:

The wine was drunk.

Note, however, the colloquial *They drank the wine* in which *they* has no specific reference. French speakers, on the other hand, seem to prefer use of an indefinite *on* when specific agent is not expressed, thereby keeping the sentence active:

On a bu le vin.

The sentence *Le vin a été bu,* which is the closest counterpart to the English passive, given above, is possible in French but not preferred stylistically.

Although differences in stylistic use of rules are relevant to a CA, it is difficult to discuss them. Since style in language, like women's fashions in the Western World, can change unpredictably, whatever we say about preferences for certain rules is subject to revision. We shall have to content ourselves with general observations. Robert B. Kaplan (1967, pp. 10-16), for example, has observed that his Arabic-speaking students of English appear to prefer certain devices of conjoining sentences over others. Thus the sentences

> The boy was here   He drank the milk.

are more frequently conjoined with *and:*

> The boy was here, and he drank the milk.

than they are in any other way, e.g.,

> The boy who was here drank the milk.

Kaplan, who is acquainted with style in Arabic, ascribes this choice of conjoining to one of those preferred in Arabic.

Another reason why it is difficult to treat style is that any comprehensive study of it would force the analyst to go beyond the sentence into discourse structure. In fact, it appears that stylistic variance is more relevant to the combinations of sentence types in lengthy discourses than it is in the choice of rules operating within the boundaries of the sentence. Unfortunately, however, formal procedures for uncovering structures larger than the sentence and discussing them unambiguously are still in the experimental stage. One of the many problems lies in finding empirical justification for the claims made by some that style somehow reflects either a culturally conditioned view of reality or certain thought patterns which arise from the native speaker's cultural orientation. Bausch (1970) gives evidence that such claims are probably without foundation. It is regrettable but necessary that we forego any extensive CA of styles.

3.6 Translation as a Basis for CA

As an alternative to providing an explicit design of language for CA, some (e.g., Kirkwood 1966) have proposed that translation serve as the basis. Presumably, the procedure is to find those sentences in a language which express the same messages conveyed by a different set of sentences in another language. For example, the message of greetings is conveyed in French (as one of several possibilities) as: *Comment allez-vous?* Its translational equivalent in English would be: *How are you?* Such a procedure, if carried to its fullest extent, would eventually involve the formulation of some general model of language design. The sentence *J'ai lu un livre* in French not only conveys the same message as the English sentence *I have read a book,* but it also has much the same grammatical structure. It is inevitable that our interests would shift from the equivalences of message to a consideration of the form of the sentences which convey the messages. In doing so, the postulation of a common deep structure would become a minimal requirement. Perhaps it would be best to think of translation as a technique to initiate CA rather than as a replacement for grammatical formulation.

3.7 Topics for Discussion

1. The notion that languages share a deep universal structure which can be interpreted on the surface in any number of ways underlies the work of many linguists, although it may be only implicitly stated. The following excerpt is from Herbert Kufner (1962, p. 77):

> . . . quite apart from the semantics of individual words or groups of words there exist in our two languages [i.e., English and German] different sets of *compulsory semantic categories,* and a description of the structure of these semantic categories and how they differ will prove helpful to our students. Sometimes it is difficult to draw the line between grammatical and semantic categories, particularly in an investigation of this sort which deals with two languages concurrently. If we were to describe only German, there is little doubt that the subjunctive, for example, should be dealt with under the heading of grammatical categories. But since English does not have a formal grammatical category which we might call subjunctive, it follows that most of the difficulties which our English-speaking students encounter are of a semantic nature, i.e., they have more trouble determining when and why to use a subjunctive than how to use it.

Questions: (1) Is subjunctive in Kufner's opinion an element of deep or surface grammar? (2) How do formal grammatical categories differ from compulsory semantic categories? (3) Discuss Kufner's last remark about students having more trouble knowing when and why to use a subjunctive than how to use it.

2. Stockwell, Bowen, and Martin (1965, p. 261) have the following to say about some uses of the subjunctive in Spanish:

> The choice of subjunctive/indicative in the adverbial clause (which may

replace a temporal, concessive, locative, or manner adverb) depends on the verb phrase in the constituent string. With the meaning "something still to be proved" (concessive), "something still to happen" (temporal), or "something unknown" (locative or manner), the constituent verb must be subjunctive when embedded in place of the simple adverb in the matrix string. With the meaning "something conceded" (concessive), "something that is known to have happened, to be happening, or to happen regularly" (temporal), or "something known" (locative or manner), it must be indicative.

Questions: (1) How much of the explanation is in terms of semantics? How much of it is syntactic? (2) What differences are implied in the interpretation of subjunctive compared with that of Kufner? (3) Can you reconcile Kufner's notion of semantic category with meaning as presented by Stockwell, Bowen, and Martin?

3. In theorizing about the design of the phonological component, Moulton (1968, p. 29) writes:

The linguistic units within this component are the Phonemes of the language; and they involve four different types of structure. First, there is a Paradigmatic Phonemic Structure (or a Matrix Structure) that deals with permitted combinations of Distinctive Phonological Features. It is to this structure that we appeal when, for example, we describe English /f/ as a Voiceless Labial Fricative, or English /g/ as a Voiced Velar Stop. Second, there is a Syntagmatic Phonemic Structure (or a Distributional Structure) that deals with permitted sequences of phonemes; typically, this is tied in with the linear sequence of grammatical units. It is to this structure that we appeal when, for example, we say that the cluster /ts/ may occur word-finally in English (as in *sits*), but not word-initially. Third, there is a Paradigmatic Phonetic Structure that deals in detail with the way in which abstract phonemes are realized in concrete sound. It is to this structure that we appeal when, for example, we say that English /l/ is typically more or less strongly velarized in contrast to the nonvelarized /l/ of French. Finally, there is a Syntagmatic Phonetic Structure (or an Allophonic Structure) that deals with the different ways in which a given phoneme is realized in sound in different environments. It is to this structure that we appeal when, for example, we say that English /p/ is aspirated word-initially (as in *pie*) but not after /s/ (as in *spy*).

Questions: What part of the design of language presented in this chapter corresponds to Moulton's "Paradigmatic Phonemic Structure"? What part of it corresponds to "Syntagmatic Phonemic Structure"? Discuss other differences and similarities.

3.8 Notes

1. The speakers of a language may come to a consensus about the use of certain rules in the expression of specific concepts. From the set of choices agreed upon by the speakers emerge the so-called grammatical norms of a language. In a manner of speaking, then, grammatical norms are stylistic choices of rules which have been fixed over a period of time. The preference for the *on* construction over the passive in contemporary French, for example, is identified as one of the grammatical norms of that language. Norms may also be set by legislation, in which case the speakers may or may not respect them. Witness the uneven influence on actual usage by the language academies of Italy, France, and Spain.

2. Although a contrastive study of the grammatical norms of two languages would have, as its background, a CA of the grammatical systems (or idealized competences, in our definition) of the languages in question, it is a study more akin to style.

3.9 Background Readings

1. On semantics: Fodor and Katz (1964); Bolinger (1965); Chafe (1970a).
2. On the phonological component: Chomsky and Halle (1968).
3. On the nature of phonological rules: Harms (1968).
4. On universals: Greenberg (1963); Bach and Harms (1968).
5. On syntax: Langendoen (1969).
6. On deep and surface structure, case grammar: Fillmore (1968); Goldin (1968).

Chapter 4

THE SYNTACTIC COMPONENT

As we take up the syntactic component in detail, we advise the reader that much of what will be said about syntactic universals and specificities is highly speculative. Speculation, however, is necessary if we are to develop a viable procedure for contrasting languages. Happily, some psychological and physiological support is starting to emerge for some of our speculations. Part of this chapter will be devoted to a brief report of the research and findings from other disciplines which corroborate our postulations.

To begin, we shall place some rather severe restrictions on what is to be considered syntactic rather than semantic or phonological. Under the heading syntax, we are therefore concerned with rules and categories (primes) of arrangement. In its most primitive sense, the syntactic component comprises the basic ways in which man builds the forms of language and then varies them to fill specific needs of communication. The sentence, for example, is a convenient abstraction to make of human language because it enables us to discuss a good deal of how man puts his thoughts together. Upon investigating the particulars of sentence, we find that other units and rules of syntactic arrangement suggest themselves. We find also that to explain the surface arrangements of language requires mention to be made of semantics and sound. (N.B. We do not equate semantics with meaning. Semantics is part of meaning, but meaning in language comprises much more. Syntactic structuring is meaningful as well because, without it, messages cannot be understood.)

Wherever reference to semantic elements is required, we shall speak of semantic projection. Grammatical gender, for example, is a projected category of semantic features with varying degrees of pervasiveness in the syntax of a specific language. Presumably, all languages would count among their semantics something called natural gender reference. Some languages project natural gender, together with other semantic features such as animateness, into the syntactic component. (More will be said about gender in chapter 5, on semantic projection.) Number, another category with syntactic relevance, derives from several possible semantic feature groupings, for example, those shown in Table 4.1.

Table 4.1   Derivation of number from semantic feature groupings

Projected Syntactic Category	Semantics Involved
Singular/plural	One vs. more than one
Singular/dual/plural	One vs. two vs. more than two
Singular/dual/paucal/plural	One vs. two vs. a few vs. many

The work of several theorists points in the same direction of limitation on the basic elements of syntax. Fillmore (1968) argues strongly for a universal set of syntactic primes consisting of S(entence), M(odality), V(erb), P(roposition), and a series of case distinctions. Bach, in the same volume which contains Fillmore's paper, speaks of "terms, contentives, operators, variables and sentences" as universals while excluding nouns, verbs, and adjectives (Bach 1968, pp. 91-122). Whatever is postulated for the syntactic base, the purposes of contrasting languages are best served by keeping deep syntax as uninvolved as possible. As a rule, languages tend to be more differentiated as one approaches their surface structures. The projection of semantic features contributes greatly to that differentiation.

Psychological support for the separation of syntax and semantics can be found in the work of several experimenters. George J. Suci, to name but one of them, has employed what he calls a "probe-latency technique" to study the reactions of his subjects to the relationship between words (Suci 1969). One result of his experimentation is that individuals seem to interpret syntactic structuring independently of semantics. (See also Lenneberg 1967, p. 30, regarding kinds of aphasia which may affect syntactic arrangement. If such illnesses are suffered universally by men, with the same symptoms, then the parts of language affected must be universally shared.)

4.1 Syntactic Primes

Syntactic primes, or base categories as they are sometimes called, identify the fundamental classes of syntactic arrangement. They constitute the class of substantive universals (section 2.5). In discussing such universals, one must avoid descriptive terms that imply the limitations placed upon them in particular languages. For this reason, terms like "noun" and "verb" which suggest the formal restraints of Indo-European languages are not used to label substantive universals. In proposing the following primes, we have relied heavily on the work of Charles J. Fillmore (1968) and to some extent on that of Emmon Bach (1968). Some adjustments have been made in the terminology and a few amplifications are suggested for some of the categories. Cases are relevant to both syntax and semantics. The arrangements of nouns and verbs which result from the presence of certain cases are within the realm of syntax, while the specific functions they perform (e.g., agentive, instrumental, and dative) have to be semantically defined.

The SENTENCE stands as the most encompassing of all syntactic primes. While there have been attempts at positing larger units of discourse (see, for example, Gleason 1968), the SENTENCE remains the largest workable unit. The formulation of its structure must be general enough to encompass all arrangements of grammatical elements which are permissible in a language. The actual number of elements in a sentence is, of course, dictated by the surface rules of a particular language, the type of discourse in which the sentence occurs, the disposition of the speaker, and the extent of the need for information. Universally, the sentence will include some sort of verbal element which is either made explicit or kept implicit in its deep structure. The number of nounlike elements present in a sentence is optional, as we shall see below.

We interpret the sentence as having two main constituents: MODALITY and PROPOSITION. The former comprises elements that have to do with the setting of the sentence, i.e., its time reference, whether or not it is negative and/or a question, and the aspect of its action (repetitive, completive, etc.) PROPOSITION has to do with the nounlike and verblike elements of the sentence and the interdependencies of these elements. Fillmore (1968, p. 23) gives the following explanation of MODALITY and PROPOSITION:

> In the basic structure of sentences, then, we find what might be called the "proposition", a tenseless set of relationships involving verbs and nouns (and embedded sentences, if there are any), separated from what might be called the "modality" constituent. This latter will include such modalities on the sentence-as-a-whole as negation, tense, mood, and aspect.

(How intonation is involved with modality is still undecided. The most workable solution might prove to be an association of intonational elements with what is called the "illocutionary force" of the sentence and, as such, more connected with the context in which the sentence is uttered than with its constituent parts. It is also possible that some of the intonational adjustments in the sentence derive from the modality. Questions in many languages may be formed by changing the intonational contour of the sentence rather than by the addition of grammatical elements. Because of the elusiveness of intonation, our discussion of it will center about the most basic of its qualities.)

In seeking a term that would suggest the verbal qualities of one of the main constituents of PROPOSITION, without implying the morphological and syntactic restrictions of any particular language, we concluded that VERBOID would best serve our purposes. We coin the term in keeping with both scientific and linguistic traditions (cf. Hockett's 1958 *contoid, vocoid* as labels for consonantlike and vowellike sounds). The suffix *-oid* (as in *celluloid*) conveys the general meaning of form or shape without limitation to a precise shape or form. Since the VERBOID is the syntactic prime which encompasses all verbal functions regardless of how these functions are expressed in the surface grammar of a language, we find this neologism a useful one. Later on, we shall see how verboids are associated with semantic features which result in a remarkable variety of surface phenomena. For the present, it is sufficient to observe that verboids plot the relationships between the nounlike elements of the sentence.

The other major constituent of PROPOSITION is CASE CATEGORY. In Fillmore's words (1968, p. 24), CASE CATEGORIES comprise

> a set of universal, presumably innate, concepts which identify certain types of judgments human beings are capable of making about the events

that are going on around them, judgments about such matters as who did it, who it happened to, and what got changed.

As we have pointed out above, the specifications of such judgments are considered as being elements of semantics rather than of syntax. This step is necessary since we have interpreted syntax as concerned strictly with arrangement of grammatical entities.

Adhering to this point of view entails a reexamination of the notion that syntax is the central component of language, motivating semantics. The less radical claim would be that syntactic primes are not realized as the particular grammatical forms of a language without the incorporation of semantic elements. What motivates what seems to be a moot point, at the very least. "Agent," "instrumental," "locative," and other case notions that Fillmore posits are specified in the syntactic prime CASE CATEGORY via a set of early projection rules from semantics. The convention for writing these specifications is the same as that used for attaching any semantic or phonological features to rules, namely,

CASE CATEGORY $_{[agent]}$

Syntactically, the CASE CATEGORIES contain a CASE MARKER (CM) and a NAME. The CASE MARKER is a convention of deep structure which underlies surface prepositions, case inflections, and other similar grammatical forms. It may even be deleted in the surface structure, e.g., the CM realized as *by* (with agent in English) in

The roast was carved by father.

and deleted in

Father carved the roast.

NAME is to "noun" what VERBOID is to "verb." That is to say, NAME is the syntactic prime which represents man's universal need to label objects, ideas, and sentiments which are subject to his cognitive powers. The term "noun" would have been too suggestive of the surface restrictions of particular languages. Contrasting languages also makes it apparent that the semantic features can vary extensively that are grouped together as NAMES. To understand the processes of naming in a particular language requires an intimate knowledge of how that language fits the society in which it is spoken.

While still inconclusive as evidence for the reality of the syntactic primes we have posited in this chapter, the research of those who work in allied fields provides some interesting parallels to the relational nature or "commentary" of our VERBOID and the topical characteristics of NAME. The psychologist Jerome S. Bruner (1967-68, pp. 61 ff.) is one who finds "topic" and "comment" to be basic in cognition. Citing the work of U. Neisser (1967) and Ye. N. Sokolov (1963), Bruner finds the following analog to topic (or NAME in our terms) and comment (VERBOID) in information processing (pp. 61-62):

> Neisser . . . distinguishes *focal* attention from a more diffuse aspect of sensing, and takes the constructionist view that we organize events through syntheses of successive focal attendings. Each instance of focal attention may be conceived as a comment on a topic, an extraction of a feature from a more general sensory input. For his part, Sokolov notes that in the orienting response we attend to a deviation from a "neural model" of some steady state on which we have been fixing over time. When the deviation is at some critical level adequate for activating a system of extrapolatory neurons, we attend or orient. The deviation in some feature of the event is, in effect, the comment, the topic being the steady state neurally represented.

Bruner goes on to find additional corroboration for the distinction between topic and comment in the way that man, as opposed to other animals, differentiates his manual prehension into a power grip and a precision grip. Unlike prosimians, who make very little distinction between power and precision in grasping, and the apes, who, being further along the evolutionary scale, have developed precision, man asymmetrically uses one hand for power (usually the left) and the other for precision. Being able to hold objects firmly with one hand while working on them with the other has doubtlessly been of far-reaching consequences not only for man's toolmaking but also for his language. The connection between man's ability to grasp objects with one hand and work on them with the other and the proposed basic dichotomy in language of naming and expressing relationships may not be as farfetched as it would appear at first glance.

It has also been observed that about the time that children develop hand preference (21-36 months) they also begin to speak (Lenneberg 1967, Table 4.8, p. 180). Although the specific neurophysiological correlates of language are unknown, Eric Lenneberg (1967, p. 175) sees an intimate connection between man's language and other aspects of his being:

> The development of language, also a species-specific phenomenon, is related physiologically, structurally, and developmentally to the other two typically human characteristics, cerebral dominance and maturational history. Language is not an arbitrarily adopted behavior, facilitated by acci-

dentally fortunate anatomical arrangements in the oral cavity and larynx, but an activity which develops harmoniously by necessary integration of neuronal and skeletal structures and by reciprocal adaptation of various physiological processes.

For references to work on topic and comment, see McNeill (in press) and de Laguna (1963). Hockett (1958) uses the terms topic and comment to refer to the constituents of only one type of construction. We can assume that Hockett's use of these terms is relevant to the surface patterns of language.

There is no doubt that in time to come more will be known about the psychological and physiological correlates to human language. The work done by cognitive anthropologists is also significant in clarifying the sociocultural context of language (see, for example, Tyler 1969). The linguist, in positing language universals such as the syntactic primes discussed here, contributes theoretical constructs which are open to corroboration by other researchers and which can spur future investigations into man's physical and social being along meaningful paths. Finding out how much of language is innately endowed and how much of it is acquired by experience is of particular importance to the language instructor who is, so to speak, on the front line of application. If it can be said that languages differ only with regard to what can be acquired through experience, the work of contrasting them becomes a minimum requirement for promoting new experiences through formal strategies of instruction. No claim is made, however, that contrastive rules are isomorphic with the manner in which teaching materials are to be presented. As we shall see in chapter 8, there are many ways to cover new experiential fields.

4.2 Universal Syntactic Ordering Rules

Robert Longacre (1965) has likened the sentence to a play. The modality is its setting; the proposition its plot; the verboid is its action, which involves names as actors. There are assorted props such as case markers which help to specify the role each name plays in the unfolding of the plot. Although such an analogy is anecdotal, it is helpful in understanding the basic ways in which sentence elements can be ordered. Of the two types of ordering, hierarchical and linear, only the hierarchical one is imposed on the base elements of syntax. For example, the output of two deep structure rules of the type

$$A \rightarrow B, C \quad \text{and} \quad B \rightarrow D, E$$

could be represented by any one of four tree diagrams (Figure 4.1).

Linear restrictions are seen to arise in the surface structure of language. Some linguists (e.g., Chomsky 1965) have proposed that both hierarchical

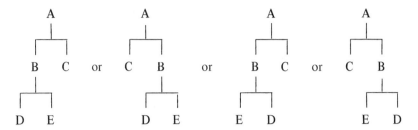

Figure 4.1 Representations of deep structure rules A, B

and linear order are relevant to deep structure. Such a proposal would appear to save steps since fewer rules would be required theoretically to generate the surface forms of a language. There are, however, several factors that lead us to deny the requirement of a linear restriction in deep structure. First of all, a linear order worked out for the deep structure of one language may not be appropriate to any other. The same deep structure restrictions of linear order that would save us steps in generating the surface forms of one language may lead to complications in yielding the surface forms of another. Then, if deep structure is to reflect a fixed and unambiguous set of logical relationships underlying all languages, how do we decide which linear order is the correct one? What part would linear restriction play in this very abstract level of grammar? A fixed linear order in deep structure would imply that languages which follow it closely on the surface are more logical than those which do not. There is no reason to assume that a language which places the subject of its sentences before the predicate is proceeding according to a more logical order than one which puts the predicate first. Finally, the assumption that deep structure has a fixed order helps in no way to explain why this order should vary in the surface structure.

The first of the universal ordering rules is:

1.   S(ENTENCE)→M(ODALITY), P(ROPOSITION)

That is to say, SENTENCES are understood as having a modality and a proposition as their major constituents, but not necessarily in that sequence. The ways in which these constituents are realized in any particular language include placing the modality first in the sentence, placing it at the end, and building it into one of the specifications of the proposition. The reader will note that the rules given here follow very closely those of Fillmore (1968). Among all of the proposals regarding syntactic ordering rules in the deep structure, Fillmore's is especially workable because of its extreme simplicity. Our departures from Fillmore's proposal will be noted wherever relevant. First of all, Fillmore does not go into much detail with regard to modality.

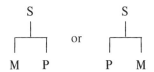

Figure 4.2 Deep structure diagrams with Modality and Proposition

We must assume, therefore, that it is to be specified as any element having reference to setting: time, aspect, and so on. Thus, we would go directly to a semantic projection rule which incorporates elements of semantics such as the following:

2.   M→[time, aspect, Q, negation, etc.]

We could also consider such elements as [time, aspect, etc.] to be syntactic, rather than semantic, but that would be begging the question. The important point here is that the specification of modality involves such features, regardless of what we call them.

PROPOSITION is rewritten as VERBOID and a string of CASE CATEGORIES. Here again, Fillmore specifies the CASE CATEGORIES as "agent." "instrumental," "dative," etc., which, because of their composition, should probably be considered semantic rather than syntactic units of arrangement. For this reason, we write our syntactic ordering rule as follows:

3.   P(ROPOSITION)→V(ERBOID), C(ASE) CAT(EGORY) $_{1...x}$

where CASE CATEGORY can be any number of specified categories.

The next rule concerns the constituents of CASE CATEGORY, which are NAME and a CASE MARKER:

4.   C(ASE) CAT(EGORY)→NAME, C(ASE) M(ARKER)

Fillmore accounts for the embedding of sentences by deriving them from the objective CASE CATEGORY. We would include this information in a

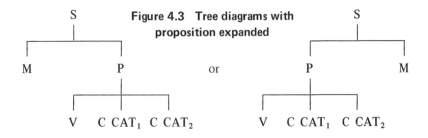

Figure 4.3 Tree diagrams with proposition expanded

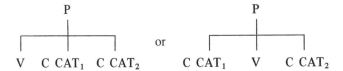

Figure 4.4 Detail of expanded proposition

rule like the following semantic projection:

5.   NAME→S, where C CAT is specified as [objective]

To illustrate how these rules are applied, we can draw tree diagrams, and from now on we will use abbreviations. To tree diagrams such as those of Figure 4.2 we can attach expansions of P(ROPOSITION) as in Figure 4.3 with, of course, the same lack of linear ordering of each of the constituents of P (Figure 4.4).

Taking the sample sentences given in chapter 3, we can draw one deep structure tree diagram for all of them (Figure 4.5).

1. John drank the wine.
2. The wine was drunk by John.
3. Jean a bu le vin.
4. Le vin a été bu par Jean.

The tree gives the information that the time reference is past, the action is drinking, the objective of that action is wine, and the agent doing the action

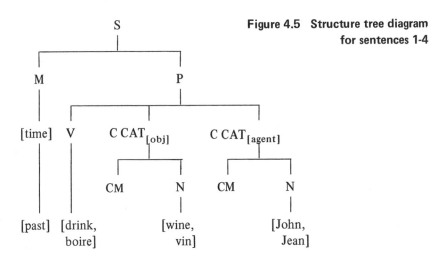

Figure 4.5 Structure tree diagram for sentences 1-4

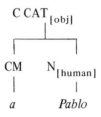

Figure 4.6   Modification for deep structure tree

is someone named John. The specific ordering rules of English and French will place either the objective or the agent case category in the subject slot. They will also specify that the CM of agent is deleted if it is the subject and that the CM of the objective case category is deleted regardless of whether it is the subject or not. The required use of the auxiliary *be* and *être* will also be explained via the specific ordering rules of English and French. The same deep structure tree diagram holds for the sentences

  5. The wine was drunk.   6. On a bu le vin.

in which no particular agent is given. The two languages contrast in how they handle unspecified agents. English prefers the passive while French generates a dummy agent, *on,* and keeps the sentence active. It is obvious that the form taken by the sentence in the particular grammar of a language depends to a large extent on the kinds of semantic projection which are made. It is also clear that such expressions as active and passive or even subject, predicate, and object (as opposed to objective) are restricted to the surface grammar of a language. Some grammatical forms, such as *on* in French and *it* in English, will prove to be necessitated by the surface grammar and therefore are not universal in their composition.

Varying the semantic specification of elements in the deep structure can trigger variations in the surface arrangement of sentence constituents. In Spanish, for example, the sentence

  Juan bebió el vino.

is very much like its English and French counterparts discussed above. However, if we stipulate that the objective case category be specified as a human noun and keep the sentence an active one, the case marker of the objective must be realized as the preposition *a:*

  Juan golpeó a Pablo.   John hit Paul.

The deep structure tree in Figure 4.5 is modified accordingly in Figure 4.6.

Looking at other languages, we find that active-passive can be built in any number of ways. In Javanese (a language having several formally distinguished levels of style—here we have picked the one called ngoko), the use of an active marker prefixed to the verb and the lack of an explicit case marker for the agent are characteristics of active sentences. The sentence

Sardi lagi ngunḍuh katès.

translates as 'Sardi [proper name] is picking a pawpaw [fruit].' *Sardi* is the agent, and *ng-* marks the verb as an active one. If, on the other hand, we would want to use a passive sentence (and we would in Javanese, if the objective is to be marked as definite, i.e., *katèsé, 'the* pawpaw'), then a passive marker is prefixed to the verb: *di- + unḍuh,* and the case marker of the agent is realized as *karo:*

Katèsé lagi diunḍuh karo Sardi.

Differing from English, French, and Spanish, the passive sentence in Javanese may vary in its surface arrangement. The following are all possible in addition to the one given above:

Katèsé karo Sardi lagi diunḍuh.   Lagi diunḍuh karo Sardi katèsé.
Karo Sardi lagi diunḍuh katèsé.   Lagi diunḍuh katèsé karo Sardi.
Karo Sardi katèsé lagi diunḍuh.

They are listed in diminishing order of stylistic preference, with the last being the least preferred. The deep structure for the active sentence and all six of the passive ones is given in Figure 4.7 (with case markers, definitizer, and verbal inflection left unspecified).

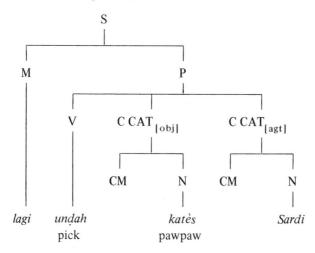

Figure 4.7 Deep structure for Javanese sentences

Tagalog, too, has active and passive sentences in its surface grammar. The active type, however, has two possibilities. The agent may occupy the first position in the sentence, e.g., *Si Juan* (John) in

Si Juan ay kumain ng tinapay.   John ate the bread.

or it may be placed after the objective, as in

Kumain ng tinapay si Juan.

Note that when the subject precedes the verb, as in the first example above, a verbal connector is required: *ay,* as it is in passive sentences:

Ang tinapay ai kinain ni Juan.   The bread was eaten by John.

Note also that in the passive sentence the objective (*tinapay*) is definitized (accompanied by *ang*). *Si,* which accompanied *Juan* as agent in the active sentences, is a subject marker which is used for proper names and is absent from the passive sentence. The verb is inflected accordingly.

Fillmore, in discussing the kinds of deep structure case relationships that must exist, posits the following in addition to that of the agent and the objective:

instrumental   factitive   dative   locative

There may well be others, but we agree with Fillmore that these case relationships must exist and that others may be added. Each particular language has its own idiosyncratic way of realizing case relationships in their surface structures. Much has to do with how case markers are handled. Types range from those languages which realize them as prepositions, or similar types of disjointed markers, with either a minimum or a total absence of inflection of name categories. This type is represented by English and Chinese. Others, like Turkish, rely almost totally on inflectional markers. Still others have a combination of prepositions and inflection. An example of the third group is German. It has also been illustrated by Fillmore that the lexicon of a language is intimately connected with the kinds of case categories that exist. Verbs, especially, can be discussed in terms of *case frames* in which are specified the case relationships with which they are involved. We can classify the English verb *cook,* for example, in terms of its association with an objective (food, meat, vegetables, etc.) and secondarily with an agent (the chef, mother, etc.) The case frame for *cook* is written as follows:

+ [_____ O (A)]

We shall have more to say about such matters in chapter 6, The Structure of Lexicon.

Another feature of the universal syntactic ordering rules, which is just

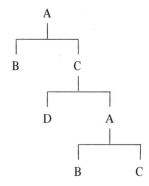

Figure 4.8 Embedded constituent

touched upon by Fillmore, is *embedding*. Simply put, embedding is the generation of a constituent which is of a higher hierarchical order than the one that immediately dominates it. As an illustration, consider a constituent A which generates BC but which can also be generated from C. The rules which we would write for such a situation would take the form:

A→BC   and   C→D(A)

and application of these rules would produce the tree diagram of Figure 4.8. The sentence

Henry wants John to study the lesson.

contains an embedded sentence. (To simplify our discussion, we shall assume that only sentences can be embedded in the deep structure.) The embedded part can be identified as *John to study the lesson.* (Henry wants *something. What* does he want? He wants *John to study the lesson.*) The embedded S is generated from the case category marked as objective in the deep structure (Figure 4.9). We observe that the realizational rules of English may vary with regard to the ordering of sentence elements in the embedded part. In the sentence diagrammed in Figure 4.9, the embedding contains an infinitive *to study.* In other sentences like

Henry wishes that John would study the lesson.

the embedded part contains an auxiliary *would* and is connected to the remainder of the sentence by a subordinator *that.* Some languages, like French, realize similar embeddings only with the subordinator type:

Henri veut que Jean étudie la leçon.
Henry wants John to study the lesson.

Languages also employ various kinds of deletion in realizing such sentences. When the agent of the embedded sentence is the same as the agent of the

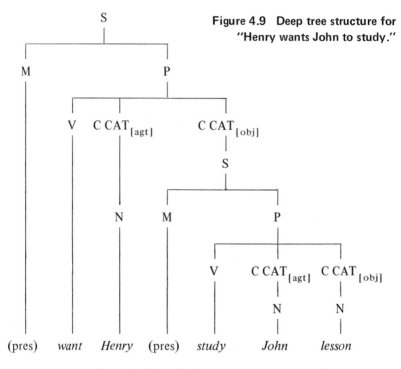

Figure 4.9   Deep tree structure for "Henry wants John to study."

sentence containing the embedding (called the *matrix* sentence), the agent is not repeated, thus:

Not: *Henry wanted Henry to study the lesson.
But: Henry wanted to study the lesson.

The same type of deletion is found in French:

Henri a voulu étudier la leçon.

Embedding of sentences in the objective case category accounts for several kinds of surface pattern in languages.

Consider the English sentences   It was John who did it.
                                    John was the one who did it.
                                    The one who did it was John.

and the Spanish sentences   Fue Juan quien lo hizo.
                                  Juan fue quien lo hizo.
                                  El que lo hizo fue Juan.

All six would derive from a deep structure in which a sentence is embedded in

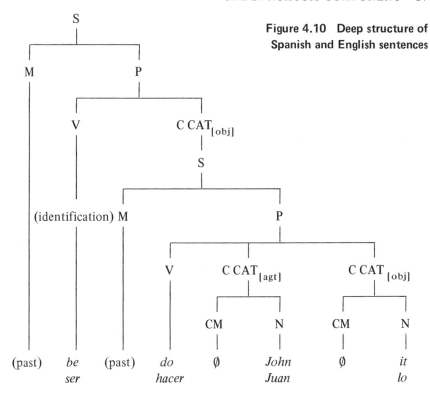

Figure 4.10 Deep structure of Spanish and English sentences

the objective case category (Figure 4.10). Note that the embedded sentence has the same hierarchical structure as the French sentence *Jean a bu le vin* discussed earlier in this chapter. That sentence could also have been embedded in a structure of the type discussed here, e.g., *C'était Jean qui a bu le vin.*

In realizing the English sentences, we observe that a dummy subject *it* is generated if some part of the embedded sentence is not made the subject of the surface sentence. The dummy *it* is not to be confused with the *it* which derives from the objective case category. The objective *it*, like its Spanish counterpart *lo*, results from transformations which can also specify semantic features. Thus

It was John who *painted the house.*
  (did it)
It was John who did *his homework.*
  (it)
Fue Juan quien hizo *el proyecto.*
  (lo)

If the agent of the embedded sentence is made the subject of the surface sentence, its place in the predicate is taken by the expression *the one who.* The agent may also be placed in the predicate, in which case *the one who* becomes the subject.   The Spanish counterparts allow for positioning the agent subject either before or after the verb: *Fue Juan* or *Juan fue.* If the agent is made the predicate of the surface sentence, Spanish employs a personal pronoun *él* plus the subordinated clause *que lo hizo. Quien* is not used in such constructions.   One could go into much greater detail on the ways in which languages realize deep structures.   In this section, however, our focus has been on the ways in which a variety of language-specific surface structures can be traced back to a set of universal ordering rules.   We have only hinted at the ways in which deep structures are generated.   The basic points are (1) universal ordering rules specify a hierarchical order, i.e., modality and proposition are contained in sentence, but no linear order (subject before predicate, etc.), and (2) embedding is found whereby constituents may be reintroduced in the generation process.   In regard to this last point, only sentence is interpreted as open to embedding.   Fillmore imposes also the restriction that all embedded sentences derive from the objective case category.   We have not challenged this position, but it is altogether possible that some embedding occurs in modality also, generating thereby sentences with concessive or resultative classes: *If it rains* (modality), *I'll take my umbrella* (main proposition).   In a manner of speaking, the *if* clause does set the conditions of time and aspect for the main proposition.

4.3 Specific Syntactic Ordering Rules

Any number of permissible linear sequences of syntactic primes are found among the world's languages.   In addition, various devices of agreement and deletion are used.   If we interpret adjectives as deriving from sentences embedded in the objective case category, we can investigate the ways in which each language orders them.   In Swahili, for example, the noun being modified occupies the initial position (see chapter 5 for further discussion of adjectives and other parts of speech) with semantic categories of adjectives following in a prescribed order.   The Swahili expression

viti vidogo viwili

means 'two small chairs,' *viti* meaning 'chairs' (stem: *kiti*, 'chair'), *vidogo*, 'small,' and *viwili*, 'two.'   The linear order is, then, the opposite of that of English.   The agreement of elements as to number is assured by the repetition.

of *vi,* the plural marker. The singular, 'one small chair,' would involve repetition of *ki,* the singular marker:

kiti kidogo kimoja   (-moja, singular)

The agreement as to number (and incidentally as to class of noun stem) continues with other sentence elements. The sentence *Two small chairs are enough* is rendered:

Viti vidogo viwili vinatosha.   (-*natosha,* 'enough')

In learning a foreign language, students often have trouble with the ordering of syntactic elements. Thai students of English, for example, have difficulty remembering which constituent of the following is being modified and which is the modifier:

watch pocket vs. pocket watch
flower garden vs. garden flower

Only the order modified + modifier is permitted in Thai. While a simple inversion rule of the type

(Thai) modified + modifier → (English) modifier + modified

should be easy to learn, the Thai-speaking student is very likely confused by those English expressions where the same words are either modifier or modified. Apparently it would be much easier for the Thai to remember that *watch pocket* means a 'pocket for watches' (in the reverse order of his own language) if English did not also have the expression *pocket watch.*

A survey of the kinds of borrowings from English into the Romance languages shows how a difference in linear ordering can reshape the original expression. The French expressions *le smoking, le night,* or the Spanish one, *el water,* are the results of borrowing from English in which the element which was the modifier has come to be the element modified:

smoking jacket	night club	water closet
le smoking	le night	el water

Such phenomena are not surprising when we remember that the usual linear order of elements in French and Spanish noun phrases is noun + adjective.

There are other kinds of specific ordering rules which have relevance in contrasting languages, but we shall not take them up at this time. An understanding of them is, perhaps, best achieved by inspecting the kinds of semantic projection found among languages (see chapter 5).

4.4 Problems

1. Irish

Data:	Is asal é.	It is an ass.
	Is capall é.	It is a horse.
	Is fear Peadar.	Peter is a man.
	Is ainmhí gabhar.	A goat is an animal.

Glosses:	asal—ass	fear—man
	capall—horse	ainmhí—animal
	é—it	gabhar—goat
	is—is	

Questions: (1) What part or parts of the sentences can be considered as realizations of the case categories? (2) What happens to the case markers? (3) In what ways are the realizations of such sentences like their counterparts in English? (4) In what ways are they different? Notice in particular the placement of the verbal element.

2. Spanish and English

The sentence in English *Old men and women were dancing* is ambiguous while the Spanish sentences

Bailaban los viejos y las viejas.   and   Bailaban los viejos y las mujeres.

do not have the same kind of ambiguity. Offer some explanation as to (1) why the English sentence is ambiguous and (2) how the Spanish sentences are not. (3) Can you find some sentences in Spanish which have an ambiguity not paralleled by English?

3. Contrast two languages of your choice with regard to placement of verbal element and case categories in sentences. Discuss also how case markers are realized.

4. Korean

The sentence *Leesi-nun cha-rul satsumnida* means 'Mr. Lee bought a car.' The deep structure tree diagram of this sentence is given in Figure 4.11.

Describe the realizational rules which convert the deep structure elements into the specific linear sequence of Korean. Discuss the ways in which these rules differ from those which would produce a counterpart in English.

4.5 Notes

1. A matter to be explored in detail is the feasibility of using the expressions of mathematical logic to describe deep structure. Logical terms like *property* and *relation* may very well be analogous to *topic* and *comment* or

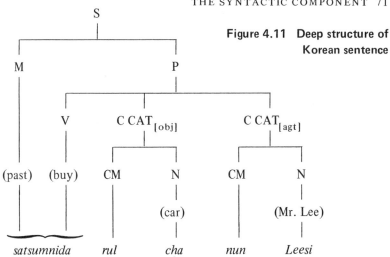

Figure 4.11 Deep structure of Korean sentence

VERBOID and NAME in grammar. Since the statements of logic are language independent but also expressible in any human language, they may provide the framework for future discussion of the conceptual structure that underlies all human languages.

2. The invariable cases of deep structure as envisioned by Fillmore (1968, pp. 24-25), and as utilized in this book, are to be kept distinct from the inflected surface cases of various languages. Locative, as an example of one of these case relationships, identifies the spatial orientation which is understandable by all humans and which turns up in a number of different language-specific ways. In German, the underlying locative case is expressed in the form of at least two distinct surface cases, e.g., dative with expressions of position or rest (*Ich stehe vor dem Haus*, 'I am standing in front of the house') and accusative, when some motion is implied by the verb (*Der Lehrer setzt sich vor die Klasse*, 'The teacher sits down in front of the class').

4.6 Background Readings

1. On an alternative view of deep structure: Langendoen (1969).

2. On innately endowed aspects of language and culture:
   Tyler (1969); Bruner (1967-68); Lenneberg (1967).

3. For an application of case grammar to Spanish: Goldin (1968).

Chapter 5

SEMANTIC PROJECTION

It is difficult, if not impossible to discuss the syntax of a particular language without referring to elements of semantics. Already in the last chapter, we had to involve semantic features like [human] and [definite] just to illustrate some basic arrangements of syntactic elements. To go beyond the most elementary of syntactic ordering rules requires that we consider the effects that various semantic features have on the form that particular grammars take. It is useful to presuppose that each language selects from the universal stock of semantic features in its own ways and that the particular selection of features in each language depends, to a large extent, on how speakers interpret their environment and structure the communities in which they live. Language does not exist in a social vacuum. The honorifics of Japanese, for example, reflect the need its speakers feel for addressing each other according to age, standing in society, kinship, sex, and so on. For this reason, we must keep in mind, as we provide an explicit statement of such elements of language, that they represent one solution to a problem of communication.

If language is to be considered a system of arbitrary signs, its arbitrariness derives from the fact that there are many solutions to the same problems of communication. In studying semantic projection, we come to grips with these problems and their possible solutions.

Understanding that language is for communication leads us also to view the semantic component, with its features, as relevant to meaning in a way different from that of the syntactic component. All of language means something. It is only a convention that some of that meaning is most easily thought of as discrete units or features, while another part of meaning, equally important, derives from arrangement. If speakers of a language could not agree on a limited number of syntactic arrangements in which to order semantic features, communication would be impossible. In fact, we observe that pidgin languages, arising from the massive confrontation of persons speaking different languages, usually develop conventions of syntactic arrangement which are not the same as the native languages of the persons using these pidgin languages. Semantic features, on the other hand, are convenient ways in which to characterize focal points of interest in man's interpretation of his being, community, and universe. It is under the title of semantic projection that we shall discuss the ways in which these semantic features interact with syntax to form the surface structure of particular languages.

Depending on the language, specific semantic features have a more or less pervasive effect on the syntax. The feature [definite], for example, gives rise in English and other languages to a special syntactic element known as the definite article, e.g., *the bread, the man, the woman,* etc. Other languages, like Russian, have no such element in their syntax. (We must not come to the conclusion, however, that languages lacking definite articles cannot definitize their nouns. See section 5.9.) We notice that each language interprets the two universal categories of NAME and VERBOID in unique ways, depending on the semantic features that "fill" them. We also observe that the lexicon of a language, its words, are agglomerates of semantic features arranged in some sort of hierarchical fashion. For such reasons, it is useful to discuss the role of semantic features in separate states: (1) how they affect the realizational rules of a language, (2) how they are projected into general syntactical categories, and (3) how each language builds its lexicon. The first and the second stages are discussed in this chapter, with the entire sixth chapter devoted to the structure of lexicon.

5.1 Elements of Particular Grammar

The surface patterns of sentences peculiar to a language have led grammarians to devise language-specific techniques to discuss these patterns. Patterns lead to paradigms and paradigms to so-called parts of speech. The Latin sentence

Amo puellam.	I love the girl.

for example, provides the framework for establishing lists of verbal forms which can substitute for *amo,* 'I love':

Amas puellam.	You (singular) love the girl.
Amat puellam.	He loves the girl.
Amamus puellam.	We love the girl.
Amatis puellam.	You (plural) love the girl.
Amant puellam.	They love the girl.

If we exhaust the forms of the verb which occur in Latin, we arrive at a paradigm of that verb. We may also investigate the many forms of the noun *puella,* 'girl,' e.g.,

Puella amat puerum.	The girl loves the boy.
Puer dat panem *puellae.*	The boy gives bread to the girl.
Etc.	

and produce a paradigm of the noun *puella.*

Turning our attention to concatenations of words, we would also investigate the ways in which sentence elements can be substituted for each other. In this way, English grammarians have found it useful to label the major constituents of a surface sentence in English as subject and predicate. The sentence

The boy loves the girl.

has as its subject *the boy* and as its predicate *loves the girl.* It is well to point out, however, that the kind of branching tree diagram that one could produce for such a sentence, showing its surface (linear) arrangement, would reveal only the patterns of substitution (see Figure 5.1). In other words, the specification that surface sentences have a subject and a predicate means only that one could replace each constituent with other constituents and produce grammatically acceptable sentences. Thus, the subject constituent *the boy* could could be replaced by *my brother, her mother, the little old toymaker,* and so on, but not by constituents like *it is a fact that* or *having been accepted.* Features of surface arrangement do not, as a result, relate directly to deep structure relationships. The subject in the following sentences is identical, but the deep structures are quite different:

The professor likes his students.   The professor is liked by his students.

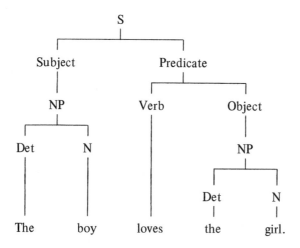

Figure 5.1 Surface tree

Determining whether a sentence is active or passive is a matter appropriately delegated to considerations of particular languages. If we are to apply the notions of active and passive at all, we must first supply a definition of what characterizes each type of sentence in a particular language. In English, active sentences are those in which an agentive, human or nonhuman, can be the subject:

The neighbor's son broke the window.   (human agent)
The shock broke the window.   (nonhuman agent)

Passive sentences, on the other hand, have objective nouns as subjects and either agentives or instrumentals optionally specified:

The window was broken.
The window was broken by the neighbor's son.
The window was broken by the shock.
The window was broken {by/with} a hammer.

Hammer in the last example can be taken either as a nonhuman agentive (in which case it did not involve a human agent) or as an instrument (implying a human wielder). The distinction between nonhuman agent and instrument often comes up in legal situations where lawyers try to determine whether a weapon was discharged spontaneously or with the intervention of a human agent. As has been pointed out by Fillmore (1968) and by Goldin (1968), sentences may also contain both an instrumental and an agentive:

The window was broken by the neighbor's son with a hammer.

A different set of surface restrictions is found in French, where the use of a passive usually involves a specified agent, human or nonhuman:

La fenêtre a été brisée par le fils du voisin.　　　(human agent)
La fenêtre a été brisée par le choc.　　　(nonhuman agent)

If, however, the impersonal *on* is used as subject, the reference must be only to human agent:

On a brisé la fenêtre.

meaning that somebody (not something) has broken the window. To express instrument wielded by someone unknown, one would say

On a brisé la fenêtre avec un marteau.　　Somebody broke the window
　　　　　　　　　　　　　　　　　　　　　　with a hammer.

When the relationship of agent to the action of the sentence is considered to be remote or not relevant, the reflexive is often used in French:

La fenêtre s'est brisée.

which roughly translates into English as *The window broke.*

Spanish imposes yet another kind of restriction on passive sentences. There are two auxiliary verbs in Spanish, *ser* and *estar,* equivalent to English *be.* In sentences that specify agent, the use of *ser* is required.

La casa es pintada por el propietario.
The house is painted by the owner.

It is observed, however, that the active sentence is stylistically preferred over the passive when the agent is specified. When it is not, a reflexive is used:

El propietario pinta la casa.　　　(specified agent)
Se pinta la casa.　　　(unspecified agent)

In modern standard Arabic, use of the passive carries with it the stipulation that the agent *cannot* be specified:

Kataba Saliim lkitaab.　　　Selim wrote the book.
Kutiba lkitaab.　　　The book was written.
　　　　　　　　　　　　　(kataba = wrote; kutiba = was written)

In other languages, like Japanese, it is highly debatable that one should use the active-passive distinction. However, if we can associate certain features, such as use of subject markers and verbal forms with active and passive, we can pair sentences like the following ones in Japanese:

Kinjono kodomotachiga uchino kodomo o ijimeta.	The children of the neighborhood treated our child badly.
Uchino kodomoga kinjono kodomotachini ijimerareta.	Our child was treated badly by the children of the neighborhood.

In the first one, the active sentence, an emphasis is placed on the agent:

kinjono kodomotachiga	literally, 'neighborhood's children'

while the second sentence, the passive one, shifts the emphasis to the action:

ijimerareta	was treated badly

thereby conveying an increased degree of parental concern for the child. As in English, the agent in the passive sentence, *kinjono kodomatachini,* could have been omitted.

5.2 Dummy Subjects

In the surface patterns of some languages there is a requirement that the subject "slot" be filled in all declarative sentences. At the same time, such languages will allow objective case categories to be realized either in the subject or in the predicate slot. The sentence

That the wine turned to vinegar is no surprise.

has an objective (resulting from an embedded S) *that the wine turned to vinegar* as the subject. The following sentence has the same constituent placed in the predicate:

It is no surprise that the wine turned to vinegar.

The realizational rules of English contain the instruction that a "dummy" subject in the form of *it* be generated when such constituents are in the predicate. Langendoen (1969) explains the presence of *it* in such sentences as resulting from "extraposition" of the subject phrase. This explanation is necessary only if (1) deep structure elements are interpreted as having a linearly fixed order and (2) that order has objectives in the subject slot. In view of the great variation in this respect found among the world's languages, such restrictions on the deep structure seem to be unfounded. (See Goldin 1968 for a further defense of our position.) In Figure 5.2 is a proposed deep struc-ture tree for both sentences.

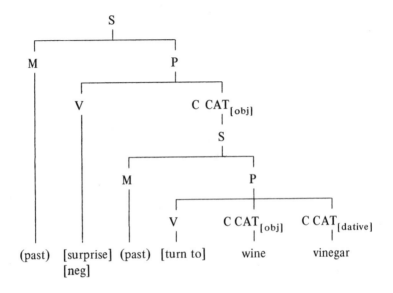

Figure 5.2 Deep structure for sample sentences with and without dummy subject

Italian, to take a language which does not have anything like the dummy *it*, simply allows the objective to be placed in either subject or predicate slot. The following are Italian equivalents to the two English sentences given above (*che il vino sia diventato aceto* is the objective):

Non è sorprendente che il vino sia diventato aceto.

Che il vino sia diventato aceto non è sorprendente.

French, on the other hand, has dummy subjects. The following sentences are French counterparts to our English and Italian samples:

Il n'est pas surprenant que le vin se transforme en vinaigre.

Que le vin se transforme en vinaigre n'est pas surprenant.

The French dummy *il* is often replaced by another, *ce*, in colloquial style:

Ce n'est pas surprenant que le vin se transforme en vinaigre.

An investigation of German suggests a pattern similar but not identical to that of English, with the use of *es* as a dummy subject:

Es wundert mich nicht, daß der Wein zu Essig geworden ist.
Daß der Wein zu Essig geworden ist, wundert mich nicht.

In colloquial German, a pronoun, *das,* accompanies the verb when the objective precedes it:

Daß der Wein zu Essig geworden ist, das wundert mich nicht.

Other dummy words like English *there* (not to be confused with the adverb of location) are not so easily identified as surface subjects:

There arrived an old man at the inn.   Once there lived a giant.

In such sentences, the noun phrase (or optionally a pronominal) which occurs in the predicate slot is traditionally considered to be the subject (e.g., *an old man, a giant*). Yet, it appears that the surface restrictions having to do with dummy *it* apply as well to dummy *there*. The only difference seems to be that the objective case category must contain a nominal (or pronominal) constituent rather than an embedded sentence. The use of *it* in such a context would be clearly ungrammatical. In contrast to English, German employs the same dummy regardless of whether the objective in the predicate slot is an embedded sentence or a nominal constituent. Note the use of *es* in the following:

Es kam ein alter Mann.   There came an old man.
Es lebte einmal ein Riese.   Once there lived a giant.

Yet another contrast with English can be found in the omission of the dummy subject in sentences which have the objective in the predicate slot but which are also initiated with an adverb (in this case *trotzdem*):

Trotzdem kam nichts dabei heraus.
In spite of that, nothing came of it.

Without the initial adverb, *es* would be used:

Es kam nichts dabei heraus.   Nothing came of it.

The use of *there* in sentences expressing existence or presence parallels similar patterns in other languages:

English: *There is* a man in space.
Italian: *C'è* un uomo nello spazio.
French: *Il y a* un homme dans l'espace.

Such sentences are apparently generated from a deep structure something like the one illustrated in Figure 5.3.

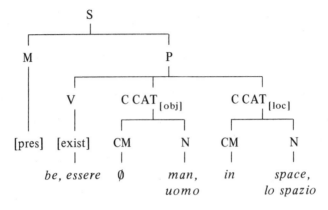

Figure 5.3 Deep structure of sentences expressing 'existence'

Although each of the languages mentioned above has its own particular way in realizing this deep structure, the linear order of subject + predicate in the surface structure is common to all of them. Both Italian and English make the verb agree with the expressed number of the predicated objective:

Italian: Ci *sono* uomini nello spazio.
English: There *are* men in space.

The French *il y a* is invariable:

Il y a des hommes dans l'espace.

Spanish *hay (Hay un hombre en el espacio),* Portuguese *tem,* and German *Es gibt* do not express number. Spanish *hay* and Portuguese *tem* do not contain dummy subjects in the sense given here. They should probably be considered verbs in the surface grammar.

The same deep structure given for *There is a man in space* also yields in English:

A man is in space.
In space is a man.

The second example may seem contrived in this context, but this surface pattern is often used in English in descriptive style, e.g., describing a painting:

In the background is a tree; in the foreground, a man; and so on.

5.3 The Copula

Many languages of the world, especially but not exclusively those of the Indo-European family, display a feature of surface grammar which has come to be called the *copula*. In terms of particular grammar, it is conveniently thought of as a verb. English grammar, for example, uses *be* as a copula in conjunction with expressions of time, aspect, and other features of modality that accompany the verb:

He *is* a student.
He *wasn't* a student.
He *hasn't been* a student.

That copulas arise from verboids in the deep structure is borne out by their use in realizing verbal relationships or operations such as state, identification, and definition. Compare the following expressions of state of being. Both English and Korean require a copula, while Russian does not:

John is young.
[iván maladóy]   (Russian: iván = John, maladóy = young)
[ǰānin čom ta]   (Korean: ǰānin = John, with subject marker,
                  čom = young, ta = copula)

Spanish conveys an aspectual relationship with state of being by the use of two different copulas:

María está guapa.   Maria is pretty. (i.e., at the moment, she is dressed
                     prettily or looks pretty)
María es guapa.   Maria is pretty. (i.e., she is a pretty girl)

In Chinese, there is a marker, *shr* (in romanization), which is used with intensifiers:

Hǎi-lún jyóu shr měi.   Helen is truly beautiful.

or to join one nominal construction with another:

Hǎi-lún shr měi nyǔ.   Helen is a beautiful girl.

(*měi* = 'beautiful,' *jyóu* = 'truly, exactly,' *nyú* = 'girl,' *Hǎi-lún* = 'Helen'). The marker *shr* is not used in Chinese sentences which contain only an adjective:

Hǎi-lún měi.   Helen is beautiful.

(More will be said about adjectives, nouns, and the copula as part of the discussion of parts of speech.)

C CAT

CM   N   **Figure 5.4 Expansion of CASE CATEGORY**

The use of the copula can vary also in the kinds of embeddings that languages allow. The English copula *to be* is optional in sentences like

I find it [to be] very interesting.

whereas it is not generated in German:

Ich finde es sehr interessant.

Both languages have the copula obligatorily in embeddings initiated with a relator of some sort (*that,* daß):

I find that it *is* very interesting.   Ich finde, daß es sehr interessant *ist.*

5.4 The Realization of Case Markers

Recall that case markers were given as part of the expansion of case categories in deep structure (Figure 5.4). In the Indo-European tradition of particular grammar, such case markers have been called *prepositions.* The particular preposition depends on many factors—both syntactic and semantic. If the dative is placed after the objective in the surface structure of English, for example, the case marker with the dative is realized as *to*:

I gave the book *to* John.

If the dative is placed before the objective, the case marker is not realized:

I gave John the book.

We note that the preposition for locatives in English can be either *in* or *at*:

at home   (obligatorily *at*)
in Washington   (obligatorily *in*)
in school   (optionally *in*)
at school   (optionally *at*)

The expression *at home* is unique since it alternates with *home* for location:

I'm home.   or   I'm at home.

It is obligatorily *home* (with no preposition) when used with verbs of motion:

He's going home.

The grammar of case markers presents the learner of a foreign language with some of his greatest difficulties. The reason for the learning problems is that languages persist in using the same prepositions for any number of different deep structure relationships. The English preposition *to* is used, among others, with datives:

Give this *to* John.

with destinations:

to Europe   (I'm going *to* Europe.)

German *von* is found in locatives, *von dem Dorf,* 'from the village'; in objectives, *wir sprechen von Robert,* 'we're talking about Robert'; etc. Furthermore, the rules for realization can vary greatly even among closely related languages. Compare, for example, English *home* or *at home* with German *zu Hause* and *nach Hause:*

Er bleibt zu Hause.   He stays home.   or   He stays at home.
Er geht nach Hause.   He goes home.

In some languages, case markers turn up as inflectional endings on noun stems or as some kind of bound form. In many languages, inflections and prepositions work together to express deep relationships. Latin is an example of a language with such an arrangement. The preposition *ab* means 'from' and is used together with the ablative inflection of the noun:

ab Romā   from Rome

The preposition *ad*, 'to,' requires the accusative:

ad Romam   to Rome

The inflections, however, could often be used without the separate prepositions; thus *Romā* meant 'from Rome,' and *Romam,* 'to Rome.' The interrelationship between prepositions and nominal inflections has been expressed in particular grammar (especially in the European tradition) as government. Thus, in German, it is said that the prepositions *aus, bei, mit, nach, seit, von, zu* "govern" the dative case.

It is often observed that the realization of verboid affects the choice of prepositional case marker. The verb *entrer* in French, for example, requires that the case marker specifying destination be realized as *dans*:

Il est entré dans le restaurant.

whereas in English, in similar situations, a preposition is not used:

He entered the restaurant.

When the English verb *enter* has the meaning of 'to be a part of,' the preposition *into* is used:

It does not enter into the plan.   Ça n'entre pas dans le programme.

The learner of French is also faced with understanding the difference between *penser à*, 'to think of,' and *penser de*, 'to have an opinion about.' Of course if he is a speaker of Italian, he should have no difficulty with these verbs since his own language makes a comparable distinction.

5.5 Phrasal Verbs

In the surface structure of some languages, prepositions occur without being associated with any expressed name category. English has many instances:

Let's *put* the kettle *on*.   *Pick* the paper *up*.

Other languages have them as well, as, for instance, Italian:

Mettiamo su la pentola.   Let's put the kettle on.

Butta giù le pietre.   Throw down the stones.

(The Italian verbs are *metter su,* 'put on,' and *buttar giù,* 'throw down.') In discussing the phenomenon in English grammar, the term "phrasal verb" has been used, with the prepositional part functioning in some way like an adverb. Such phrasal verbs can be distinguished in English from other verbs insofar as the prepositional part can occur either immediately following the verb or after the objective:

Pick up the paper.   or   Pick the paper up.

while prepositions associated with explicit case categories cannot:

Sit on the chair.   but not   *Sit the chair on.

There are several ways in which to explain how phrasal verbs arise in the surface grammar of English. One is that certain case categories (expressed as preposition + noun) have come to be closely associated with verbs. When this happens, the noun of the case category is deleted. We can find some historical evidence to support this explanation. In expressions like *put the kettle on*, a noun or a noun phrase might very well have previously accompanied the preposition *on*, e.g., *put the kettle on the fire* (or *on the stove*). Such a deletion can be illustrated in the form of a transformation operating on the tree structure (Figure 5.5).

In many phrasal verbs, however, it would be difficult to ascertain what particular noun had been deleted, as in *call up, turn off*. As a result, it may be preferable to think of the prepositional part of phrasal verbs as deriving from case categories in which the name element has simply not been realized. In this way, we need not postulate an underlying noun or noun phrase for each preposition in a phrasal verb. (Note that English has also developed compounded phrasal verbs, such as *drop on by* and *come on in.*)

Deletion does function, however, in avoiding the repetition of identical noun phrases in expressions like

Are you coming *from* or going *to* Rome?

for: Are you coming *from* Rome or going *to* Rome?

He walked *up* and *down* the street.

for: He walked *up* the street and *down* the street.

In contrast to English, German has sets of phrasal verbs, some of which allow separation of preposition and others do not. Thus, *übersetzen* (with loud stress on *über* is comprised of *über*, 'over,' and the verb *setzen*, 'sit.' It means 'to leap over' or 'to cross,' and the prepositional element can be separated

Ich setze über.

The same verb, with the loud stress on *setzen* has the meaning of 'to translate' or 'to transpose' and is not separable in two parts:

Ich übersetze.

The separability versus the nonseparability of preposition reflects the historical derivation of the verb, to a large extent. In any event, the explanation of how phrasal verbs are derived in German would be similar to that of English.

5.6 Verboids as Verbs

As we have said earlier (Chapter 4), it is convenient to think of verboids as those elements which set the plot of the sentence, thereby establishing the relationships among the nominal elements. An idea of some of these relationships can be gotten by considering sentences which involve the copula in their surface structures. We pick the copula because it is the least charged with semantic features. The following sentences illustrate verbal relationships such as state of being, inherent quality, identity, and one of a set:

Mary is beautiful. (state of being, inherent quality)

Mary is a beauty. (one of a set)

Mary is Beauty [i.e., beauty personified]. (identity)

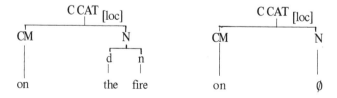

Figure 5.5 Deletion of N node

In languages like Spanish, state of being and inherent quality are distinguished by the use of different copulas:

María está guapa. (state of being)

María es guapa. (inherent quality)

In English, state of being is often expressed with the verb *look*, as in

Mary looks beautiful [today].

Even when verbs are invested with specific semantic features, they retain their relational power. In the particular grammars of many languages, it is useful to classify verbs in terms of their relational qualities. Thus, we speak of transitive and intransitive verbs, depending on the kinds of case categories with which they interact. The verb *bring* in English involves a potential objective, agent, and dative and is called transitive, while *sleep* does not seem to permit an agent or an objective and is therefore called intransitive. Verbs of motion (a subclass of intransitives) are often singled out for different grammatical treatment in the surface structure of a language. In Italian (and to some extent in French and German also), such verbs require the use of an auxiliary different from that of transitive verbs, e.g.,

Sono andato alla stazione.

I have gone to the station. (with aux. *essere*)

Ho mangiato una pera.

I have eaten a pear. (with aux. *avere*)

It is, however, difficult to ascribe to the verb many features which would be universally valid. The following excerpt from the writings of Benjamin Lee Whorf (1941; p. 215) explains the problem most eloquently:

> If it be said that "strike, turn, run", are verbs because they denote temporary or short-lasting events, i.e., actions, why then is "fist" a noun? It also is a temporary event. Why are "lightning, spark, wave, eddy, pulsation, flame, storm, phase, cycle, spasm, noise, emotion" nouns? They are temporary events. If "man" and "house" are nouns because they are long-lasting and stable events, i.e., things, what then are "keep, adhere, extend, project, continue, persist, grow, dwell", and so on doing among the verbs? If it be objected that "possess, adhere" are verbs because they are stable relationships rather than stable percepts, why then should "equilibrium, pressure, current, peace, group, nation, society, tribe, sister," or any kinship term be among the nouns? It will be found that an "event" to us means "what our language classes as a verb" or something analogized therefrom.

One could have added to Whorf's examples those situations in which nouns are built from verbs and vice versa: *beauty-beautify, organize-organ-*

ization, etc. Some linguists, e. g., Lakoff and Postal, have even postulated a relationship between adjectives and verbs, calling the former a subclass of the latter. Yet, as we shall see, adjectives and nouns in the particular grammars of many languages also share properties.

If we are to avoid the difficulties of explanation brought on by Whorf, it appears that we shall have to distinguish sharply between the semantics of relational function and that of experiential interrelation. What intrinsically defines a verb is its sets of relationships among the case categories of a sentence. Verbs are incidentally defined in terms of those semantic features which the particular language associates with experience. The English verb *beautify,* for example, has the intrinsic verbal properties of other transitive verbs and the incidental semantic features of the noun *beauty.* Of course, pairs like *beauty* and *beautify* are not always encountered in the particular grammar of a language and therefore it is not always clear that we can separate relational properties from experiential ones. Yet we must keep in mind that verbs are quite unlike nouns because their basic role in the sentence is quite different. If this approach is correct, then we would specify both the experiential and the relational features of verboids in the deep structure (see Figure 5.6).

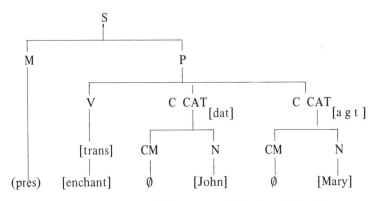

Figure 5.6 Tree with feature specification of V node

The tree in Figure 5.6 illustrates how V would have to be specified as [transitive] with all the relational properties it entails and then invested with the specific experientially derived semantic features associated with [enchant, enchantment, etc.] . The surface forms of the sentence would include

Mary enchanted John.   John was enchanted by Mary.

In keeping with Whorf, we recognize that each language makes its own decisions as to which semantic features to associate to nouns and verbs.

5.7 Adjectivization

Many languages have developed forms which grammarians customarily label as adjectives. Most recently among transformational linguists, there is agreement that adjectives are really a subclass of verbs (see, for example, Ross 1967, Lakoff 1965). It has been observed that verbs and adjectives in English share several patterns. Some adjectives, like some verbs, can be made imperatives, while others cannot:

    run! (verb)   be polite! (adj.)

but not, according to these transformationalists:

    resemble!   be swarthy!

(It could be argued, however, that the adjectives *fat* and *pregnant*, which would not occur with the imperative *be*, could be used with the verb *get: get fat!, get pregnant!* As one colleague pointed out, there seems to be nothing wrong with saying: "Stay in the sun, then. Be swarthy. See if I care!"). Also, some adjectives, like some verbs, are used in connection with animate subjects, e.g.,

> The wrestler hoped for a quick victory.
> *The driveway hoped for a quick victory.
> The wrestler was despondent.
> *The driveway was despondent.

Presumably, the underlying structure of expressions like *the red book* or sentences like *The book is red* is something like the one illustrated in Figure 5.7, where V is marked [+ adj], which may generate a copula in the surface grammar of English, or may not, if the sentence is embedded in a larger one, e. g.,

    The red book is on the table.

We do not assign a specific case to the case category because it is one of the moot points involved in the derivation of adjectives. Before we offer our own opinions, we observe also that many languages interrelate adjectives having to do with colors and verbs: *yellow* (that soap yellows clothes), *black/blacken* (they blackened their hair), etc. Recalling Whorf's observations, we must make a distinction between what a language specifies semantically in each category and the categories themselves. As far as the deep structure and the universal categories are concerned, it is inconsequential that *beautify* or *finalize* are verbs since many languages could be found where there are no counterparts to them. If we are contrasting English with any other language, however, we should know how English "fills" its verbs and nouns.

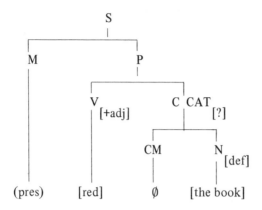

Figure 5.7 Deep structure for "The book is red."

Before the transformational treatment of adjectives, structural linguists concerned themselves with distinguishing between adjectives and nouns. Harris and Fries applied what they called "testing frames" to separate words like *ugly, beautiful* and *pretty* from others like *ugliness* and *beauty*. Adjectives were those words which could be inflected in or associated with degrees of comparison: *ugly, uglier, ugliest* or *beautiful, more beautiful, most beautiful* but not *ugliness, more ugliness, most ugliness* in sentences like: She is more _____ than Helen. (The use of *more* and *most* with nouns in sentences like: *I found more ugliness in the city* is not considered to be part of the paradigm since such comparisons seem to be at the level of Sentence, e.g., *I found more ugliness there than I did here.*) Such a testing frame was not totally successful. While some nouns, such as *friend* proved to be different from adjectives like *friendly* in: *She was more a friend* (or: *more of a friend*)/ *she was more friendly*, other nouns like *man* and *woman* were not so easily distinguished: John is *more man* than his brother (or: John is *more of a man*), Helen is *more woman* than Mary (or: Helen is *more of a woman* than Mary).

In applying the technique of the testing frame to Italian, we (Di Pietro 1963) found that so-called nouns and adjectives can be so similar as to question their separation. Although *amico* 'friend' is traditionally thought of as a noun and *giovane* 'young' as an adjective, one would be hard put to show that they differ syntactically:

un giovane	a youth
un amico	a friend
un amico giovane	a young friend
un giovane amico	a young friend
or: a youth who is a friend	

In comparative constructions, one has:

Maria è più donna di sua sorella.

Mary is more woman than her sister.

Maria è più giovane di sua sorella.

Mary is younger than her sister.

Just as it could be argued that adjectives are subclasses of verbs, it could also be maintained that adjectives are really types of nouns. To support the second claim, one could find many examples in all of the Romance languages. Even if we were to remain within the confines of English, we still would want to find a way to encorporate in our explanation of adjectives the ways in which they may function as nouns:

The good and the bad. *and* Ivan the terrible.

and the obvious relationships with nouns through derivation:

beauty — beautiful   ugliness — ugly

At this point, it seems that the only way in which to integrate both the nominal and the verbal qualities of adjectives is to recognize that adjectives function totally within the confines of surface grammar and in some languages they may arise from either verboids or case categories. English is one of those languages with both nominal and verbal adjectives. To the first group belong adjectives like *young, beautiful, old;* to the second, *enchanted, awakened,* and any form with other verbal properties.

The deep structure for nominal adjectives would be something like that in Figure 5.8. In it we extend Fillmore's notion of dative to include the situation in which beings or objects are affected by the addition of semantic elements. Fillmore would, of course, object since he follows Postal in calling all adjectives subsets of verbs. He has not demonstrated, however, that such an analysis as the one given here is not equally viable and perhaps more applicable to contrasting languages. The deep structure in Figure 5.8 is schematized to show: (1) that the verboid can express at least four different relationships, (2) that nominal adjectives derive from objectives, and (3) how the objective is realized in the surface grammar of English depends on the relation expressed by the verboid. The possible surface sentences include:

The princess is beautiful. (state of being, inherent quality)

The princess is a beauty. (one of a set)

The princess is Beauty. (identity or personify)

Deletion of the verboid can lead to such expressions as:

The beautiful princess.

It is unknown as to how many languages derive their adjectives in a manner similar to this pattern in English. There can be several variations in the surface realizations. In Russian, for example, both nouns and adjectives are associated with datives without the aid of an expressed copula:

[mál'chik mólod]	The boy is young. (in experience)
[mál'chik molodoy]	The boy is young. (in years)
[mal'chik yúnosha]	The boy is a youth.

If we call adjectives [molod] and [molodoy] verbs, then we would also have to call the noun [yúnosha] a verb. If we keep to our notion of the verbal function as one of interrelating, we can say that it is the linear ordering or positioning of surface nouns and adjectives which reflects this particular kind of interrelationship. In languages like Latin where linear surface order is not so important, such relationships are expressed by keeping the nouns and adjectives in the (surface) nominative case inflection:

Petrus vetus (est).	Peter is old.
Est vetus Petrus	Peter is old.
Vetus est Petrus.	Peter is old.
Petrus miles est.	Peter is a soldier.
Miles est Petrus.	Peter is a soldier.
Est miles Petrus.	Peter is a soldier.

The other source for adjectives is the verboid itself:

The princess charmed the prince.

The prince is charmed.

The charmed prince.

(The last example results from an embedded sentence.) The underlying tree would be something like the one in Figure 5.9.

We could also have obtained:

The charming princess.

if we had chosen to associate the verbal adjective with the agentive. Whereas transitive verbs like *charm* in English can be adjectivized with either *-ed* or *-ing*, intransitives like *sleep* are only of the second type:

Sleeping beauty.

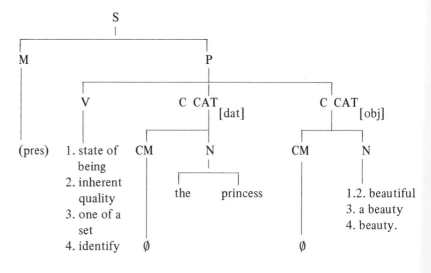

Figure 5.8 Deep structure tree with nominal adjectives

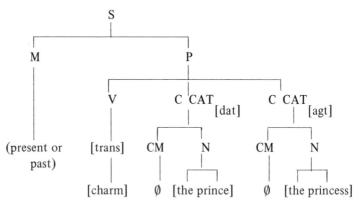

The dative category is so marked in keeping with Fillmore's restriction that all human recipients of action are dative rather than objective.

Figure 5.9 Deep structure tree with verbal adjectives

In French, two surface forms are opposed to the present participle of English. They both have the inflectional ending *-ant* , but the form which the French grammarians consider to be an *adjectif verbal* agrees in gender and number with the noun it modifies. In this way, the expression:

    Deux hommes pensants (adj.)   two thinking men
is distinct from:
    Deux hommes pensant ...(v.)   two men, thinking ...

There is far more to be said about adjectives in the languages of the world. What we have attempted here is a glimpse into how such forms arise in the grammar of a language. The reader must keep in mind that adjectivization is a language-specific matter and there may be languages where any discussion of adjectives would be totally irrelevant. Our intention here, as elsewhere, is to give an outline and an orientation into the process of contrasting languages, rather than an exhaustive treatment of grammar.

5.8 Names as Nouns

Each language treats its names in distinct ways, according to the syntactic restrictions which it places on the semantic features associated with them. In English, for example, the types of verbal relationship into which nouns may enter and the particulars of number inflection lead to classifications such as the following: concrete nouns, abstract nouns, mass nouns, countables, etc. Overriding rules of agreement between a noun and its modifiers cause nouns in other languages to be classified as to gender or as to features like animate vs. inanimate, human vs. nonhuman, etc. (There is no implication that gender is not expressed in English but rather that it plays a role of reduced syntactic importance when compared to, say, French.) It is difficult to find a reason for this variance other than to say that each complex of speech communities representing each language finds its own things to talk about and give importance to. Indeed, an analysis of the nouns of the language as labels of artifacts and concepts is a recognized tool for anthropologists and others who wish to study the culture of a people. A cursory survey of labels for meals, for example, can reveal much about the social patterns of a people. In English we have *breakfast, brunch, lunch, snack, dinner, supper,* and *banquet* . We observe also that the actual times when these meals take place in English-speaking communities can vary considerably, along with the amount of food eaten at any of them. The terms used to label relatives reveal the kinship structure of the community. In English, for example, 'mother's brother' and 'father's brother' are both called *uncle*, whereas other languages may have different words. Nouns also reflect the changes in social structure which a community undergoes. Latin distinguished between 'mother's brother' and 'father's brother' with the words *avunculus* and *patruus*, respectively, but none of its descendants do, e.g., French *oncle* and Italian *zio*, Spanish *tio* for both. Clearly, the patriarchal structure of ancient Rome in which *avunculus* and *patruus* functioned gave way, thereby eliminating the need for separate words. Because of the complexity of such relationships, an entire chapter will be dedicated to the matter (Chapter 6, The Structure of Lexicon). We shall also be discussing (below) some of the general ways in which languages mark their nouns.

5.9 Determiners

The definite article is an element of surface structure which is not present in the particular grammar of many languages. There is no Russian counterpart, for example, to *the* in English. Other languages, like the Romance group, have definite articles but do not distinguish indefinites from the number *one*, e.g., *un livre* means either 'one book' or 'a book' in French. Such statements do not imply, however, that some languages are incapable of expressing indefiniteness or definiteness. While determiners are language specific, the capacity to definitize must surely be universal. In this book, we shall consider determiners, where they occur, as arising from the association of a semantic feature [±definiteness] to the NAME category (Figure 5.10)

CM $N_{[\pm def.]}$ **Figure 5.10 Feature specification of N node**

whereby $N_{[\pm def.]} \longrightarrow$ det + noun. In English [−def.] yields 'a,' 'an,' or ∅ (in connection with 'plural') and [+ def] gives 'the.' In some languages, the determiner serves as a convenient place to locate other elements of surface grammar, such as number, gender, and case inflection (German: *der, die, das,* and so on.) In French the indefinite article becomes the most reliable indicator of gender:

un élève, une élève   un Arabe, une Arabe

etc. Also in French, as well as in the other Romance languages, a connection between definite articles and pronouns is obvious: *le, la* in *Je donne le livre à Jean, Je le donne à Jean; Je lave la fenêtre, Je la lave.*

Using English and Portuguese as examples, we can demonstrate some of the surface restrictions that languages place on use of their determiners. In both languages, use of an adjective with a noun of profession (student, professor, plumber, etc.) requires generation of an indefinite article:

He's a good professor.   Êle é um bom professor.

Portuguese, however, does not generate an indefinite article when the noun of profession is used with no modification:

Êle é professor.

whereas English does:

He's a professor.

With the addition of number inflection, the two languages draw closer together in that neither English nor Portuguese generate an indefinite article:

Êles são professôres.   They're professors.

Portuguese again differs from English in that the plural of adjectivized noun phrases may contain the indefinite article:

Êles são uns bons professôres.   They're good professors.

The apparent contradiction in logic, i.e., pluralizing *um* to *uns,* can be explained only by recognizing that *um* is here functioning as a determiner and not as a number. French and Italian do not pluralize indefinites in this way, choosing instead a device called the partitive:

Ils sont de bons professeurs.   Sono dei professori.

(Italian has yet another rule whereby the partitive alternates with null: *Sono professori / Sono dei professori,* without adjectivization. With adjectivization, Italian more closely resembles English in that no determiner is used: *Sono buoni professori,* as English *They're good professors.*) It can also be noted that French and Italian pluralize the pronomial *one* in: *les uns et les autres* and *gli uni e gli altri,* but not the indefinite *one* as does Portuguese.

We can summarize the types of contrast between English and Portuguese with rules such as those in Table 5.1.

$$N \begin{bmatrix} + \text{def} \\ + \text{prof} \end{bmatrix} \longrightarrow \text{(Eng., Port.) def. art. + noun}$$

He is the professor.
Êle é o professor.

$$N \begin{bmatrix} -\text{def} \\ + \text{prof} \end{bmatrix} \longrightarrow \begin{cases} \text{(Eng.) indef. art + noun} \\ \text{(Port.) noun} \end{cases}$$

He is a professor.
Êle é professor.

$$N \begin{bmatrix} -\text{def} \\ + \text{prof} \end{bmatrix} \longrightarrow \text{(Eng. Port.) indef. art. +}$$
noun, accompanied by adj.

He is a good professor.
Êle é um bom professor.

Table 5.1

The definitization of nouns in languages without definite articles can be done in a number of ways. In Turkish, for example, a definitized noun in the objective requires that the case marker be realized. The sentence:

Çayi içtim.   I drank the tea.

contains the case marker *-i* (accompanying *çay* 'tea') and is distinct from:

Çay içtim.   I drank tea.

The deep structures for the two sentences are schematicized in Figures 5.11 and 5.12.

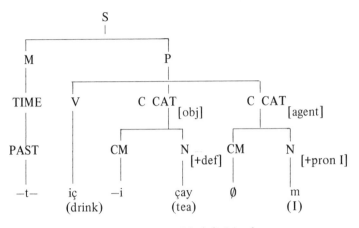

Figure 5.11 Deep structure with definitized noun

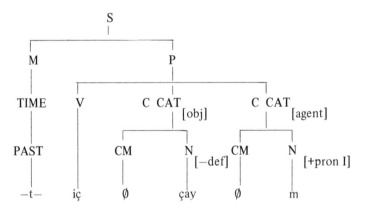

Figure 5.12 Deep structure with nondefinitized noun

The Turkish realization rule in this instance would be:

$$CM_{[obj]} \longrightarrow \begin{cases} i\,/\,\underline{\quad}N_{[+\,def]} \\ \emptyset\,/\,\underline{\quad}N_{[-\,def]} \end{cases}$$

to be read: The case marker of the objective is *i* when the noun is definitized; otherwise it is null.

5.10 Pronominalization

It has been claimed that pronouns are universally found among the world's languages (cf. Postal 1966). Whether the claim is justified or not, it is certainly a fact that the formation of pronouns or pronominalization, as it is sometimes called, is a vital part of the grammars of many languages. One could speculate that the presence of forms not requiring the full semantic specification of nouns grows out of an effort to achieve economy of expression. Without pronouns in English, the following sentences (1-3) would not be possible and would have to be replaced by sentences like 1a-3a:

(1)   John knows that he is right.
      (1a)   John knows that John is right.
(2)   John cuts himself.
      (2a)   John cuts John.
(3)   Mary and Helen put on their hats.
      (3a)   Mary and Helen put on Mary's and Helen's hats.

If pronouns like *I* and *you* were absent from English, full nouns would have to be used for reference to speaker and addressee as well. Most importantly, what would the speaker do in situations where he wishes to refer to beings or objects about which he knows very little, if he couldn't use a semantically under-specified pronoun?

Paul Postal (1966) has traced the generation of English pronouns back to at least two sources in the deep structure. In some sentences, pronouns derive from a semantic feature specification of the *name* element, e.g., [+ pronoun] in the subject of the sentence:

He arrived late.

where *he* comprises features like [+animate, +human, +male, and so on] but lacks full semantic specification underlying nouns like *John, the boy,* etc. Pronouns may also develop from the underlying structure by transformational rules when the feature specifications of multiple nouns in a sentence are identical, e.g., :

John said that John was right.   John said that he was right.

Thus, in the sentence:

John said John was right.

the two nouns *John* must refer to different persons. Along this line, we can have either backward or forward pronominalization:

The possibility that he was wrong didn't bother John.

where *he* replaces the first reference to *John* and:

The possibility that John was wrong didn't bother him.

where *him* replaces the second one.

It appears that pronouns play a role in the general process of anaphora, whereby various parts of a sentence may be deleted. Observe the following:

John said that he was going.

Q: Who said it?

A: John did. ∼ John said it. ∼ John.

In this series, the string *that he was going* is replaced by *it* and the sequence *said that he was going* was optionally replaced by *did* or totally deleted as in the answer *John*. English has yet another anaphoric device, *so*, with different uses:

If you can learn English by yourself, do *so*.

Who says you can learn it by yourself? *I* say *so*.

Our discussion of how pronominalization can differ among languages can proceed in terms of these two general aspects, namely (1) how the particular grammar of each language employs its pronouns as anaphoric devices and (2) what ranges of semantic feature specification are permitted in each language. In this chapter we shall discuss the first general aspect, leaving the second for the next chapter on lexicon.

In Spanish, when feature specifications like [+ person, + number, etc.] are present but others like [+ animate, + human, etc.] are missing, no pronoun is used: *se lava las manos* means 'somebody, male or female, washes his or her hands.' Since *manos* 'hands' refers only to humans, we know that it is not an animal that is washing. In sentences like: *Se laven.* we could not predict that the subject is human or non human, male or female, although we do know by the verbal inflection that it is plural. Of course, we must remember that such sentences may be pronounced in a context where the reference is clear.

Of especial interest with regard to contrasting languages in pronomial usage is that of the reflexive. Compare the following sentences:

John washes himself. } Juan se lava.
John washes.

John washes his hands.   Juan se lava las manos.

In English, when the agent is affecting his own person, but with no specific reference to a part of himself, a reflexive is used to realize the objective, or, optionally, the objective is entirely deleted. Spanish, on the other hand, requires a reflexive *se*. When a body part is specified, 'his hands,' for example, the deep-to-surface realization rules are the same as those with any objective in English (*John washes his hands, his clothes, his car*, etc.). In Spanish, the reflexive is required, making expression of possession in the determiner unnecessary:

Juan se lava las manos.

but

Juan lava su ropa.

The underlying tree for generating reflexives would be as illustrated in Figure 5.13.

(Admittedly, this treatment is different from that of Fillmore (1968), but it allows for interlingual contrasts in a more adequate way.) The deep-to-surface realizational rules of Spanish would include the insertion of a reflexive whenever the objective case category of the sentence embedded in objective is a physical part of the dative. This type of possession has been called "inalienable possession" and can be found in many languages:

Il se lave les mains.	French
Si lava le mani.	Italian
Er wäscht sich die Hände.	German

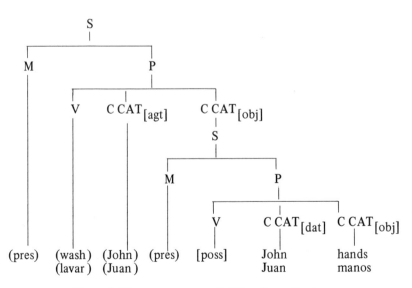

Figure 5.13 A structure underlying the reflexive

5.11 Negation

It is most probable that all human languages have some device to comment on the existence of something, the validity of an hypothesis, personal likes and dislikes, and all other matters involving affirmation and negation. It may be purely accidental, but it also appears that [negation] is more often marked among the world's languages than is [affirmation]. However the case may be, [negation] and some form of affirmation are necessary to the conducting of human affairs. It is difficult to imagine a society in which no one could express refusal or denial nor a society in which only refusal and denial are expressed, with no affirmation. A cursory investigation of negation in several languages suggests that it affects both syntactic arrangement and semantic projection. That is to say, most languages appear to have both sentence negators (English *not*, *-n't*) and specific lexical items with negation built into them (English *no one*, *nothing*, *hardly* etc.). Yet, as we shall see, there is a considerable amount of variation among languages as to the ways in which sentence negators interact with lexical negators. A series of restrictions is imposed by the particular grammar of English which prevents a surface sentence from having built into it a sentence negator along with a noun containing a negation:

No one is coming.	*not*	No one is not coming.
Nothing ever happens.	*not*	Nothing never happens.

(Double negation, of course, is found in some nonstandard varieties of English and even seems to have been the usual state of affairs in earlier stages of the language. The prescriptive rule "two negatives equal an affirmative" does not extend to such things as *neither ... nor.* Overextension does produce, among some speakers, *neither ... or.* In any event, sentences like: *I don't want nothin'* would be considered ungrammatical before they would be thought of as yielding an affirmative: *I want something.*) Italian and Spanish, in contrast to English, require a sentence negator to be used along with a lexical negator if the lexical negator is not placed first in the sentence:

Non è venuto nessuno. (Italian)	Non—sentence negator.
No vino nadie. (Spanish)	No—sentence negator.
No one came.	

If the lexical negator is advanced to first position in the sentence, no sentence negator is allowed:

Nessuno è venuto.	
Nadie vino.	(with the same meaning as above)

In the surface grammar of Russian, the positioning of the sentence negator has lexical significance. Thus:

[on nye poyexal f tu storanu]

with the negative particle [nye] before the verb, [poyexal], means 'He did not go in that direction.' Placing the negator before the locative expression [f tu storanu] 'in that direction' results in the meaning 'He went in the wrong direction':

[on poyexal nye f tu storanu]

Not only is the sentence negator used along with lexical negators in Russian, but, in expressions of existence, the lexical negator must be inflected in the genitive case, as in the following sentence:

[na vagzalye nikovo yeščo nye biło]

There was no one at the station yet.

(*nikovo*= no one, genitive case). The underlying structure is given in Figure 5.14.

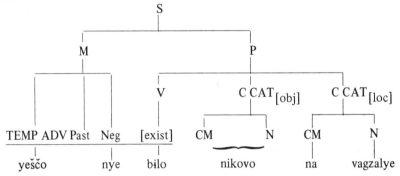

Figure 5.14 Structure underlying a Russian sentence with negation

German has a sentence negator, *nicht*, which is generally comparable to the *not* of English. There are, however, certain restrictions in German which would be of interest were we to contrast the two languages. The German sentence:

Ich habe die Bücher nicht.   I don't have the books.

is used when reference is being made to a specific set of books, discussed previously. To express the notion of 'I don't have any books' or 'I don't have books,' German requires the use of the lexically negative adjective *kein* which does not permit the use of a sentence negator:

Ich habe keine Bücher.

In the Indo-European languages, the sentence negator, together with other elements of modality, are usually placed in proximity with the verb. In German, the position of negator is usually postverbal, whereas English has more surface restrictions in this respect:

I don't study.	(attached to the auxiliary verb *do*)
I haven't any books. I don't have any books.	(attached either to *do* or to another auxiliary)
He isn't studying. He mustn't work so hard.	(attached to an auxiliary other than *do*)

(There is a vestigial positioning of negator in English which is akin to the postverbal position of German: *I lie to you not.*) Italian and Spanish place their negators before the verb, but without the use of an auxiliary:

Non vuole.   Italian
No quiere.   Spanish

French, however, has a discontinuous negator, *ne ... pas* which literally surrounds the verb:

Il ne parle pas français.

Either part of the negator may be dropped in certain instances, such as in the expression *pas du tout* 'not at all' and with certain lexical negators: *Personne n'est venu* 'No one came,' where *personne* means ' no one.'

5.12 Tag Questions

The so-called tag question found in the grammars of many languages is a device whereby the speaker asks for confirmation of the proposition of the sentence, e.g., 'haven't you?' in:

You've been studying, *haven't you?*

We propose here that such tags derive from the constituent modality in the deep structure. They are unique kinds of questions because they appear to involve an embedded sentence. We suggest the deep structure tree of Figure 5.15 for the example given above.

There are several rules which English invokes to realize tag questions. One of them has to do with the sentence negator. In simple words, if the modality of the main sentence does not specify a negator, the modality of the tag will. The converse also is true; that is, if the modality of the main sentence specifies a negator, the tag will not, e. g. :

You haven't been studying, *have you?*

The other rules of realization for tags in English include alignment of the subject with that of the main sentence. Thus, if a pronoun occurs as subject of the main sentence, it is repeated in the tag. If a noun occurs as subject, the pronoun with the same general semantic specification is placed in the tag:

John has been studying, hasn't he?

Mary has been studying, hasn't she?

Etc.

As regards the verb of the tag, the same rule operates as that of using an auxiliary with main verbs when negating them: the auxiliary *do* is used, unless the verb of the main sentence is one of a set including *be, have, must,* and *shall,* or if the main verb has already been accompanied by a verb of this set:

He has studied, hasn't he?

He should study, shouldn't he?

He studies, doesn't he?

The tense of the tag is usually dictated by the tense of the main sentence:

He studied, didn't he?

He was studying, wasn't he?

But then, there are cases like:

He will have been studying, won't he?

in which the tenses are different. In the linear ordering of the surface forms in English, the tag is placed after the main sentence, with the verb first and the subject second.

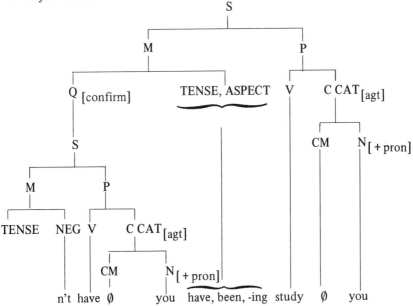

Figure 5.15 Structure underlying a sentence with a tag

English is fairly complicated when we consider the rules of realizing tags. Some languages require only an invariable form, something like the English colloquial 'hey?' (*You did it, hey?*). Other languages are between two extremes of complexity. Italian has an invariable tag, except for the negator, which has the same restrictions as does English: *Ha studiato, non è vero?* (*non è vero?* is the tag) dropping the negator in: *Non ha studiato,è vero?* The tag without the negator can have the copula deleted: *Non ha studiato, vero?*

In French, however, the tag *n'est-ce pas?* is totally invariable. If the tag is used in sentences already containing a negator and the addressee does not wish to confirm the speaker's statement, his answer includes *si* which is an alternate form of *oui* 'yes' in French:

Q: Tu n'as pas lu le livre, n'est-ce pas?
> You haven't read the book, have you?
A: Mais si, je l'ai lu!
> Yes, [that is, on the contrary] I have read it.

German has a tag *nicht wahr?* which can follow prepositions with or without a negator:

Du hast das Buch gar nicht gelesen, nicht wahr?
Du hast das Buch gelesen, nicht wahr?

Instead of a tag, German also allows the use of *odor* 'or' followed by *doch* or *nicht* in a kind of elliptic construction:

Du has das Buch gar nicht gelesen oder doch?
Du hast das Buch gelesen oder nicht?

Portuguese presents yet a different set of surface restrictions. While similar to German with regard to the negator in the tag, Portuguese also allows use of *sim?* 'yes?' or a negator with the inflected verb repeated, e.g.:

Vais trazer-me o livro, não é?
> You're going to bring me the book, aren't you?
Vais trazer-me o livro, não vais?
> You're going to bring me the book, aren't you?
Vais trazer-me o livro, sim?
> You're going to bring me the book, aren't you?

The use of *sim?* is tantamount to giving a very polite command to the addressee. An additional degree of firmness to be expected in the addressee's confirmation can be communicated by repeating the inflected verb without the negator: *Vais trazer-me o livro, vais?* (You're certaintly going to bring me the book, aren't you?) Conversely, a greater degree of uncertainty about the main proposition containing a negator is conveyed by repeating the inflected verb but not the negator: *Não vais trazer-me o livro, vais?* (You're not going to bring me the book, are you?)

Finally, the use of a tag containing a negator together with a main proposition which also has a negator is a request for confirmation:

Não vais trazer-me o livro, não ê?
You're really not going to bring me the book, are you?

5.13 Conjunction

It is most likely that all human languages employ procedures whereby constituents of the same grammatical class can be conjoined within one utterance. In English, both nouns and verbs can be so conjoined.

John and Mary are here.　　　　John danced and sang all night long.

To explain conjoining as it occurs in the various languages of the world, we shall propose that it stems from a recursion of constituents in the underlying structure. In this way, the conjoining of two nouns arises from a recursion of the NAME (N) constituent and conjoined verbs derive from a recursion of the VERBOID (V) in the deep structure (see Figure 5.16).

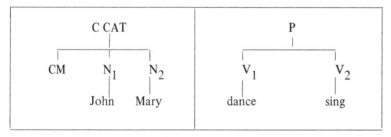

Figure 5.16 Recursions underlying conjunction

The convention we employ to signal recursion is a tagging of the constituents involved ('). In the deep rules, we would have both V and N so tagged:

$$P \longrightarrow V', \; C \; CAT$$

$$C \; CAT \longrightarrow CM, \; N'$$

It is unlikely, however, that conjoining can be explained solely in terms of syntax. A certain compatibility of semantic features is required in most instances. To give an example, the English words *faster* and *slower* cannot be conjoined even though they are of the same grammatical class. While the sentences:

John walked faster and faster.　　　　John walked slower and slower.

are grammatical, the sentence:

*John walked faster and slower.

is clearly ungrammatical. Less obvious, but equally important, are the semantic restrictions which affect verbal conjunction. It seems that in some languages, at least, verbs denoting actions that are somehow semantically connected readily admit conjunction. Observe the following English and Spanish sentences:

María *washed* and *dried* her hair.   María *se lavó* y *se secó* el pelo.

Interviews with native speakers of English and Spanish pointed to a consensus that the following variants with the pronoun object of the second verb were not as natural in either language:

Maria washed her hair and dried it. Maria se lavó el pelo y se lo secó.

In cases where the actions of the conjoined verbs were not considered to be so closely connected, either pattern of coordination (with or without the pronoun) was acceptable:

Joseph wrote the letter and mailed it.   José escribió la carta y la envió.
Joseph wrote and mailed the letter.   José escribió y envió la carta.

In the conjoining of adverbs in Spanish, the part corresponding to *-ly* in English *(-mente)* is not repeated for each adverb:

María canta suavemente.   Maria sings softly.
María canta dulcemente.   Maria sings sweetly.
María canta suave y dulcemente. Maria sings softly and sweetly.

There are various markers which languages employ in the realization of conjoined constituents, e.g., English *both ... and, either ... or, neither ... nor;* Spanish *y ... y, o ... o, ni ... ni.* Since the use of such markers (called conjunctions) must be explained as part of the realization rules of each language, they are not indicated in the deep structure.

5.14 Problems

1. Discuss the following remark of Charles Hockett (1958; p.250) in the light of our remarks on deep and surface grammar:

Languages differ as to what is on the surface and what is deep . . .. In English, as in Chinese, forms in construction with each other are usually (though not invariably) next to each other. Thus surface grammar in both languages is basically shown by linear order, while deeper connectivities between forms often cut across intervening material. But this is not true in all languages. In Latin, for example, relationships shown by linear order are largely stylistic in their semantic effects and belong in deep grammar, the surface-grammatical relationships being shown inflectionally.

In what way can we say that languages differ in their deep structure?

2. The following sentences were written by a Chinese girl studying English. What kinds of contrasts in the surface structures of English and Chinese can be surmised by her errors?

1. Students don't have bag for their book.
2. In the beginning we didn't make friend with American too much.
3. In our school the science courses have physiology, general science and physics.
4. Please you write to us when you have time.
5. Wish you have a nice celebration on Chinese New Year.

3. The following data are from Rumanian. In what way does Rumanian appear to definitize its nouns? Contrast it with English in this respect.

bằiat	boy, masculine singular	casằ	house, feminine singular
bằiatul	the boy	casa	the house
bằieți	boys	case	houses
bằieții	the boys	casele	the houses

5.15 Notes

1. Why the French should choose to derive their word for uncle from 'mother's brother' instead of 'father's brother' remains unexplained. In any event, we should not conclude that, because of this choice, France has become a matriarchal society. The present use of one term where there were previously two simply means that contemporary French society no longer considers the distinction 'father's side' / 'mother's side' so important.

2. Robinson (1970; p.283) suggests that those linguists who derive adjectives from a VP node are actually looking for a principle to allow us to delete single-branching, nonterminal nodes. Relating adjectives to verbs is really a side issue.

3. Some languages have adverbs in their surface structures. The affinity of such a class (especially the so-called adverbs of manner) with adjectives is often very evident; cf., the use of *easy* (adjective) and *easily* (adverb) in *Hunger is easy to forget. / Hunger is easily forgotten.* Compare also *hasty* and *hastily* in *Don't do anything hasty* (adj.). / *Don't do anything hastily* (adverb). There is no reason to believe that separate deep structure categories must be postulated to explain either adjectives or adverbs. Realizational rules should handle the necessary distinctions without much difficulty.

5.16 Background Readings

An extensive treatment of transformationally related sentences in Spanish contrasted with English is in Stockwell, Bowen, and Martin (1965; Chapter 9).

For an early linguistic treatment of surface and deep grammar, with its implications for contrasting languages, see Hockett (1958; Chapter 29).

Ross (1967) discusses the ways in which pronominalization operates in surface grammar. He has a view of deep structure which is different from that of Fillmore in many respects.

Ross (1969) summarizes the arguments supporting the view that adjectives and verbs belong to the same category. He goes on to treat syntactic properties of the copula with noun phrases in English.

Chapter 6

THE   STRUCTURE

OF   LEXICON

In this chapter we shall take up the ways in which languages compose their vocabularies. Each language draws in specific ways from the universal stock of semantic features in order to form its own set of word units, or idiomatic expressions. The technical term for semantic complexes is *lexemes*. The total number of lexemes comprises the *lexicon* of a language. Whatever name one might choose to give them, lexemes reflect in vital ways those elements of their physical environment, thought, and societal structure which the speakers of a language consider important enough to discuss among themselves. A good example of how a language combines semantic features to build lexemes specific to the needs of its speakers can be found in the English word *privacy*. Although other languages such as French and Spanish may share one or more of the features of this word distributed throughout the lexemes of their lexicons, neither language has a separate lexeme which combines all of the same ones pertaining to *privacy*. As a result, translations from English into French and Spanish which involve the term may be off the point entirely or limited to some peripheral feature of the word. The following set of instructions in English, with French and Spanish translations, was posted on the door of a room in a New York City hotel:

English: For complete privacy, press center button.
French: Pour fermer l'intérieur, pressez le bouton.
Spanish: Para retaimiento en el cuarto, oprima el botón.

While the message about pressing the center button is conveyed equally as well in all three languages, only English offers privacy as a reason for locking the door. The French translator simply states that the door can be locked from the inside by pressing the button, a cause-and-effect relationship which has nothing to do with privacy as a reason for locking the door. In using the word *retraimiento*, the Spanish translator conveys the idea of seclusion or aloofness and covers some of the elements of privacy but only at the expense of many other features of meaning. If the cultures which use French and Spanish had a societal convention equivalent to that of privacy in English-speaking cultures, the translator's job would have been a simple one.

Oftentimes, a need is felt to develop a concept which is like that of an alien culture. It is not infrequent, in such instances, to find that the language has borrowed the lexeme, along with the concept. Rarely, however, does the newly acquired lexeme retain all of its original semantic features. In Spain, for example, people use the word *sandwich* (pronounced ['sanduitš]) to mean only sandwiches made with slices of squared bread *(pan de molde)*, which may or may not be toasted. They retain the word *bocadillo* to refer to sandwiches consisting of a sliced roll or bun with some kind of filling and apparently never toasted. Because *bocadillo* is the older term which meant all kinds of sandwiches, the introduction of *sandwich* can be considered a specialization which takes features away from the semantic field of the former lexeme and associates new values. The operations needed to form the lexeme *sandwich* from the semantic field of *bocadillo* can be characterized in terms of feature changes:

[± square format]   [+ square format]

[− toasted]   [± toasted]

with the new alignment as follows:

bocadillo   [− square format]   sandwich   [+ square format]
            [− toasted]   [± toasted]
            etc.   etc.

In this same vein, the reader might like to speculate about the semantic makeup of *hamburger* and *hot dog* as kinds of sandwiches in English.

In much the same way, the learner of a foreign language is faced with the task of sorting out the semantic references of each lexeme in the language. Wherever possible, he will naturally assume that the semantic associations for each lexemic unit are identical to counterparts in his own language. Only part of the difficulty that the learner faces is illustrated by the three-way splitting of a semantic field in English, Spanish, and Italian. If we contrast the English word *dormitory* with its Spanish and Italian counterparts, we note that the English lexeme refers to a large building with many bedrooms, the Italian lexeme *dormitorio* is a large room with many beds, and, finally, Spanish *dormitorio* is simply a bedroom, with size and number of beds unspecified.

Discussing the differences between languages with regard to their lexicon would not be possible if we did not accept implicitly the notion of an underlying universal matrix of semantic features and a set of universal selection rules which establish the basic patterns of human cognition. That semantic features are associated in some sort of universal arrangement seems likely for several reasons. For one, man's perception of his surroundings is conditioned by his physical makeup. Having two eyes enables him to perceive depth. His sense of smell and taste lead him to distinguish odors and flavors which in turn either attract or repell him. Because of these endowed senses, all of mankind has the capacity to keep from running into objects, getting burned, or eating things which cause sickness. Another reason for positing a network of features is that at least some features seem to come in sets: [hot] and [cold]; [good] and [bad]; [wet] and [dry]; etc. It would be very difficult to define [hot], say, if it could not be opposed to [cold], or to some such term. Despite the fact that there may be many real distinctions in degree of heat measured by instruments, the human perceptive apparatus appears to operate within its own network.

Just how these universal matrices of semantic features are constructed, and what semantic primes they must include, is, at this time, totally speculative. However, the years that lie ahead will find great strides made in this area. In addition to studies of the biological nature of man's cognition (see, for example, Lenneberg 1967), anthropologists have busied themselves with the study of how the different ways in which man interprets and organizes the material world will lead to an understanding of underlying universals (see, for example, the collection of papers in Tyler 1969). Knowing, for instance, that the Koyas of southern India do not have separate words for *dew, fog, ice,* and *snow* (calling them all *mancu*), leads us to speculate about those semantic features which must be shared by the separate words in English. The semantics underlying kinship structure, color differentiation, and even food preparation have been studied with reference to different cultures (see Lounsbury 1964 and Goodenough 1965).

6.1 Problems in Semantic Analysis

The attempt by Katz and Fodor (1963) to uncover the semantics of the English word *bachelor* and to sketch the guidelines for a viable semantic theory, pointed up the great difficulty in applying formal procedures to the structure of lexicon. In his critique of Katz and Fodor, Dwight Bolinger (1965) shifts the focus from the study of individual lexemes to an investigation of how semantic features (or *markers*, as Katz and Fodor call them) are interlaced in a network. He writes (p. 564, op. cit.):

> If it is conceived as a representation of how fluent speakers behave toward anomalies as well as ambiguities, each entry will be interminable. A reasonable solution would be not to use the ordinary dictionary at all, if the model is to serve as a kind of lexical map for a natural language. Instead, it could resemble a thesaurus, where each marker would appear only once, and where each sense of a lexical item would appear as a particular path linking marker to marker.

It is in the same line of thought that we have interpreted lexemes as surface phenomena restricted to the specific grammar of each language. Each lexeme is to be interpreted as a bundle of semantic features generated by the secondary selection rules of the language in which it operates and responsive to the communicative needs of the speakers of that language.

Semantic features, since they are covert units underlying lexemes, are not open to direct observation. If we are to reach some understanding of them and of the selectional rules which operate on them, an adequate procedure will have to be devised. Of course, any claim to the universality of semantic features must be made on a completely provisorial basis. Yet, in no way is the importance of looking for semantic universals diminished by procedural difficulties. (Thus, we disagree with McCawley in his refusal to discuss universal aspects of semantics; see McCawley, 1968).

The device we will employ to postulate semantic features is admittedly a rather crude one. We first limit ourselves to what we arbitrarily consider a set of lexemes which stand somehow within the same semantic field, that is, share one or more of a number of semantic features. Next, we contrive a series of "decompositional contexts" (called "disambiguating sentences" by Katz and Fodor) which reveal one or more of the proposed semantic features. Working with limited contexts, we postulate supposed features. The postulated features are then arranged in a matrix. If the matrix is an accurate representation, each context will be accounted for. There are many shortcomings. Not the least involves the problem of separating metaphorical from nonmetaphorical uses of lexemes. There is no ready answer to this problem. It may be that the distinction between metaphorical and non-metaphorical meaning depends on how many features are to be included within the same semantic field. We can speak of *heart*, for example, in many contexts beside that of its anatomical identification (assuming that its anatomical reference is somehow more central than other references). If a speaker of English does not think of the use of *heart* in the following context as metaphorical, it may be because the entire expression is a very common one:

We have come to the *heart* of the matter.

The use of *core* or *center* for *heart* in this expression would perhaps not be ungrammatical but it would certainly be preferred less often. We might feel somewhat more easy about ascribing metaphorical status to *heart* in:

Take *heart!*
Her *heart* was broken by the tragedy of unrequited love.

because of the emotional situations in which they are said. A comprehensive statement of the mechanisms of metaphor is, regrettably, beyond the scope of the present study. What is of immediate importance here is how each language builds specific sets of semantic matrices. Most likely, types of metaphor are language specific, and what is metaphorical in one language may not be in another.

6.2 Semantic Analysis of 'meat' and 'flesh'

Following is a study of the semantic matrices underlying the English words *meat* and *flesh*. These two lexemes have been chosen for the analysis because they represent distinctions not shared by many languages of the world which have only one lexeme in the general area. A number of semantic features have been postulated in terms of the decompositional contexts which are characterized by the sentences 1-14. The first feature to be treated is [± human]. Other features are uncovered by repeating our inspection of each sentence, e.g., [± concrete, ± specific, etc.]. The labels for the features are not intended to be absolute but represent, instead, an attempt to characterize each feature adequately. Next, semantic matrices are drawn up for each lexeme and a tree is constructed as an illustration of part of the underlying semantic structure. The contrastive procedure is, then, to match *not* the lexemes *meat* and *flesh* with lexemes in other languages but rather the kinds of realizations represented by them with realizations in other languages. In this way, metaphorical and nonmetaphorical uses are lumped together, a procedure which seems to be necessary before the two uses can be separated.

Examples for the establishment of underlying semantic features for meat and flesh, with features isolated, are as follows:

[+human]
1. He got goosebumps on his flesh.
2. The spy's flesh crawled with fear.
3. The soldier suffered a flesh wound.
4. A fat person is one with a lot of flesh.
5. She was a child of his own flesh and blood.
6. Cannibals eat human flesh.
7. The sins of the flesh are many.

[−human]
8. Lions devour the flesh of many animals.
9. Freestone peaches are fleshy.
10. The English boil their meat.
11. Deer meat can tast gamy.
12. The butcher specializes in salted meats. (Note that only *meat* can be pluralized.)
13. Nut meats are fattening.
14. The philosophers got the meat of the argument.

At this point, we reinspect the decompositional contexts and extract other features:

[+human]
[+concrete]
3. The soldier suffered a flesh wound.
4. A fat person is one with a lot of flesh.
5. She was a child of his own flesh and blood.
6. Cannibals eat human flesh.

[+human]
[−concrete]
7. The sins of the flesh are many.

[−human]
[+concrete]

8.   Lions devour the flesh of many animals.
9.   Freestone peaches are fleshy. (Semantic interpretation of this type does not distinguish adjectives from nouns or verbs. Thus, *fleshy* has the same makeup as *flesh*. See Section 6.5.)
10.   The English boil their meat.
11.   Deer meat can taste gamy.
12.   The butcher specializes in salted meats.
13.   Nut meats are fattening.

[− human]
[− concrete]

14.   The philosophers got to the meat of the argument.

[+human]
[+concrete]
[+localized][1]

1.   He got goosebumps on his flesh.
2.   The spy's flesh crawled with fear.
3.   The soldier suffered a flesh wound.
6.   Cannibals eat human flesh.

[+human]
[−concrete]
[+localized]

(lacking)

[+human]
[+concrete]
[− localized]

5.   She was a child of his own flesh and blood.

[+human]
[− concrete]
[− localized]

7.   The sins of the flesh are many.

---

[1] The feature [localized] refers to occurrence of the lexeme with others having to do with location, type or other such specific qualities, e.g.,'spy's flesh' is [+localized] and 'child of his own flesh and blood' is [− localized].

[− human]
[+concrete]
[+localized]

8.   Lions eat the flesh of many animals.
9.   Freestone peaches are fleshy.
11.   Deer meat can taste gamy.
12.   The butcher specializes in salted meats.
13.   Nut meats are fattening.

[− human]
[+concrete]
[− localized]

10.   The English boil their meat.

[− human]
[+concrete]
[+localized]
[+animal]

8.   Lions devour the flesh of many animals.
11.   Deer meat can taste gamy.

[− human]
[+concrete]
[+localized]
[− animal]

9.   Freestone peaches are fleshy.
12.   The butcher specializes in salted meats.
13.   Nut meats are fattening.

[− human]
[+concrete]
[− localized]
[+animal]

10.   The English boil their meat.

[+human]
[+concrete]
[+localized]
[+internal]

4.   A fat person is one with a lot of flesh.
6.   Cannibals eat human flesh.

[+human]
[+concrete]
[+localized]
[− internal]

1. He got goosebumps on his flesh.
2. The spy's flesh crawled with fear.
3. The soldier suffered a flesh wound.

[− human]
[+concrete]
[+localized]
[+animal]
[+internal]

11. Deer meat can taste gamy.

[− human]
[+concrete]
[+localized]
[+animal]
[− internal]

8. Lions devour the flesh of many animals.

[− human]
[+concrete]
[+localized]
[− animal]
[+internal]

13. Nut meats are fattening.

[+human]
[+concrete]
[+localized]
[+internal]
[+edible]

6. Cannibals eat human flesh.

[+human]
[+concrete]
[+localized]
[+internal]
[− edible]

4.   A fat person is one with a lot of flesh.

[+human]
[+concrete]
[– specific]
[– internal]
[– edible]

5.   She was a child of his own flesh and blood.

    At this point we terminate the decompositional process for *meat* and *flesh*, reminding the reader that the labels chosen for the features are purely impressionistic and are meant primarily for purposes of illustration. It may well be that some important feature has been omitted, or that some of the features given, are inaccurate. In the absence of a thoroughgoing semantic analysis of the lexicon of English, we can do no more than postulate features and label them in some plausible way. We note that an additional semantic feature is perhaps "human or nonhuman agent." Animals usually devour the flesh of other animals while humans eat meat (the exception being cannibals who eat human flesh). We did not include such a feature because it did not seem to add any substantive clarification to the semantic field of either lexeme. Observe the pattern of coefficients in Table 6.1:

Table 6.1   Feature matrix of 'meat' and 'flesh'

	1	2	3	4	5	6	7	8	9	10	11
human	+	–	+	–	+	+	+	–	–	–	–
concrete	–	–	+	+	+	+	+	+	+	+	+
localized			–	–	+	+	+	+	+	+	+
animal								+	+	–	–
internal					+	+	–	+	–	+	–
edible					+	–	–	+			

In Figure 6.1, a tree diagram is given of how the groupings are interrelated (note that here, as well as in phonological feature analysis, +values are always placed on the left-hand branches and –values on the right hand ones). Note that there is no need to specify [+animal] if [+human] is specified, nor [+edible] if [±animal] and [+internal] are indicated. The specifications [+human, –concrete] and [–human, –concrete] make all others redundant. The eleven semantic groupings are exemplified by the following:

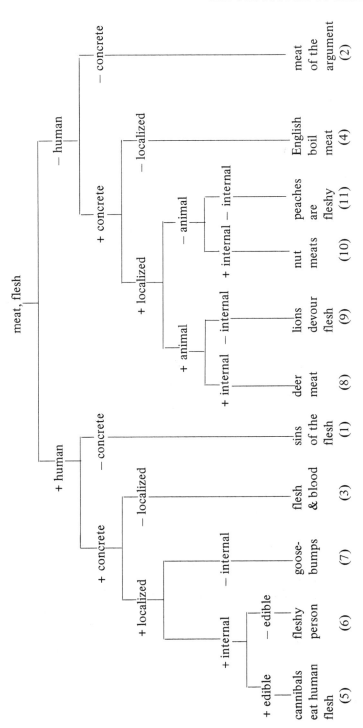

Figure 6.1 Semantic feature tree for 'meat' and 'flesh'

1. sins of the flesh
2. meat of the argument
3. child of one's own flesh and blood
4. English boil their meat
5. human flesh eaten by cannibals
6. fleshy person
7. goosebumps on one's flesh
8. deer meat
9. lions devour flesh
10. nut meats
11. peaches are fleshy

We can now proceed to contrast our postulated features and arrangements with those of other languages. In doing so, an insight is obtained into the variety of ways individual languages associate semantic features to form lexemes.

Many languages simply do not use features such as the six given for English to differentiate *meat* from *flesh*. Portuguese, German, Vietnamese, and Bengali, for example, associate the features [animal, edible, etc.] in matrices to form only one lexeme each:

Portuguese:*carne;* German: *Fleisch*; Vietnamese:*thit*; Bengali: *maŋso*.

If we employ decompositional contexts similar to those of English, we will find that various features belong to different matrices in the language we contrast with English. In French, for example,

[−human]
[+concrete]
[+edible]
[+animal]

are used to form a lexeme *viande*, while [+human] figures in another lexeme, *chair*. Thus, one says in French: *la viande salée* (salted meat) but *la chair humaine* (human flesh). It would, however, be rash to find a parallel to the English distinction between *meat* and *flesh* because another feature that is important in the formation of French *chair* is [−concrete], provided that [+human] is also present. For this reason, neither *chair* nor *viande* can be used to refer to a fleshy person. If [−human] and [−concrete] are both selected, French requires that [+specific] and [+internal] also be present and the association is with matrices underlying other lexemes. Thus, for the *meat of the argument*, one uses either *la thèse* (the thesis) or *le point* (the point) *de l'argument.* In a similar fashion, Portuguese has *razão* (reason) or *motivo* (motive),*do argumento* and Bengali has [tɔrker šarmɔrmo] , literally, the gist of the argument.

The lexemes of a language are interrelated according to its own patterns of association. Thus, French has *la chair de poule* (literally, chicken flesh) for English goosebumps or gooseflesh, keeping some parallelism between *chair* and *flesh*, while Italian has *la pelle d'oca* (or, goose skin) in which *oca* = (goose) but *pelle* is used instead of *carne* (flesh or meat). (See also German *Gänsehaut.*) Portuguese selects features for both skin and chicken: *pele de galinha*.

From the above discussion it should be obvious that a lexeme-to-lexeme comparison of languages would not be very fruitful. The learner of a foreign language, in order to effectively use the lexicon of the new language, must learn how that language associates recurrent semantic features in new and unfamiliar patterns. The learner has no automatic way to distinguish between central meanings and peripheral or secondary ones. Nor has he any way of determining universally what will be metaphorical and what will not. A minimal requirement for the teacher would apparently be some understanding of the semantic features underlying each lexeme and the associations of matrices. The decompositional contexts themselves become a teaching device to be manipulated in any number of ways (see Chapter 8, for further discussion of techniques).

6.3 Lexical Classification by Semantic Marking

Languages have various ways of grouping their lexemes into general semantic categories. In English, for example, we speak of mass nouns and count nouns, referring to whether or not the noun in question may be pluralized. *Sugar* and *milk* are thus placed in the category of mass noun, while *desk* and *chair* are countables. Some words refer only to human females: *seamstress, actress, midwife,* while others seem to be strictly male in reference: *tailor, husband, bass-baritone,* and so on. Yet another group can have reference to both: *writer, teacher, consultant.*

When a language has some surface feature which correlates frequently enough with an underlying semantic association to affect word shapes, grammarians speak of an 'inflectional category.' In this way, the distinction in number with regard to the countables yields the inflectional category of 'number' in English, with its singular/plural opposition, e.g., *desk/desks, chair/chairs.* Other languages have a category called 'gender' which centers on the [male]/[female] opposition, but which can include other semantic feature pairs such as [human]/[inhuman], [animate]/[inanimate], and [plant]/[animal]. It is interesting to note that English is not thought of as having inflectional gender because neither the appropriate deep-to-surface correlations nor the effects on word shapes are sufficiently evident. Some linguists have, however, pointed out the patterns of pronouns and nouns involving [male]/[female] features: *seamstress/she, tailor/he,* and so on (see Hockett, 1958; p. 232-233). The *lion/lioness, actor/actress, duke/duchess* type relationship is usually explained as a derivational one rather than an inflectional one. Since what we call inflection is restricted to word shapes in the surface grammar, a deep-to-surface correlation which involves more than one word stem is not usually considered to be inflectional. For this reason, 'aspect' as illustrated by: *I study, I am studying, I do study, I am about to study,* and so on, is not considered to be inflectional. The composite parts of such paradigms are usually treated separately. In Russian, aspect turns up in the form of a verbal marker, such as *pa-* 'reiterative,' and is consequently thought to be inflectional. Friedrich (1970) discusses how the Tarascan language of Mexico associates semantic features of shape with surface categories of inflection, e.g., [round], [flat], [long], which obligatorily occur with nouns. Thai is another language with 'shape' references in its surface structure. While not wishing to go too deeply into the matter of semantic marking which leads to inflectional categories in the surface structure, we shall consider briefly gender as one type. (Gender should serve as a good illustration because it is often discussed in traditional grammar books.)

Among the Indo-European languages (e.g., the Romance group and German, Russian, and Greek), nouns, pronouns, adjectives, and sometimes verbs are often marked as being 'masculine,' 'feminine,' and 'neuter' (some languages, like Polish, might even have more distinctions, involving, among others, profession and age). The marking appears in the surface structure in several ways. In Italian and Spanish, masculine nouns are often terminated with a vowel [o] and feminines with [a]. There are, of course, many exceptions. The best surface indicator of gender in German appears to be the definite article:

der Tisch	the table (masculine)
die Wand	the wall (feminine)
das Fenster	the window (neuter)

In French, the indefinite article is more indicative of gender (due to the elision which affects the vowel of the definite article):

un élève	a student (masculine)
une élève	a student (feminine)

(Cf. also *artiste, adversaire, aide, enfant, esclave,* and *hypocrite*). Another pattern noticed in languages with inflectional gender is the one involving derivational affixes. In both Italian and German, the addition of augmentative or diminuitive suffixes can change the gender of the stem: *donna* 'woman,' fem./ *donnone* 'big woman,' masc. with *-one* as an augmentative suffix in Italian, and *Frau* 'woman,' fem./ *Fräulein* 'girl,' neuter, with *-lein* as a diminuitive suffix in German. This last point also serves to illustrate how speakers of languages with inflectional gender can fluctuate between surface to surface relationships and deep to surface relationships. In German, for example, pronomial reference to *Fräulein* can either be with the neuter *es* (if the pronoun follows close upon citation of the noun) or with the feminine *sie*, which carries the semantic feature [+female]. The neuter *es*, with reference to human females, seems to be more formal in style than *sie*:

das Fräulein?	Es ist hier!
das Fräulein?	Sie is hier!

Several surface patterns can be observed with regard to gender assignments. In many languages, nouns with [+human] as one of their features function differently from those with [−human], with gender more predictable. [−human] often entails a subdivision into [+animate] and [−animate], with correlation as to surface gender more difficult. The feature [−animate] would occur in all lexemes denoting objects, artifacts, myths, and theories. What happens in the Indo-European languages with regard to [−animate] nouns is that the gender assignments appear totally random, e.g., German:

die Welt	the world (feminine)
das Fenster	the window (neuter)
der Bahnhof	the station (masculine)

contrasted with Italian:

il mondo	the world (masculine)
la finestra	the window (feminine)
la stazione	the station (feminine)

(Italian has no neuter gender.) In nouns referring to fruits and the trees that bear them, the Romance languages show a pervasive pattern whereby the tree is masculine and the fruit feminine (this pattern breaks down, with fruit names imported from other languages, e.g., Spanish *melocotón* 'peach,' masc., *melocotonero* 'peach tree,' also masc. *Pérsico* and *pérsica* follow the pattern, but they are restricted to technical, botanical usage). Some examples of the pervasive pattern are given in Table 6.2.

		French	Italian	Spanish
'apple'	fruit (fem.):	pomme	mela	manzana
	tree (masc.):	pommier	melo	manzano
'cherry'	fruit (fem.):	cerise	ciliegia	cereza
	tree (masc.):	cerisier	ciliegio	cerezo
'pear'	fruit (fem.):	poire	pera	pera
	tree (masc.):	poirier	pero	peral
'plum'	fruit (fem.):	prune	prugna	ciruela
	tree (masc.):	prunier	prugno	ciruelo

Table 6.2 Patterns of Gender Assignment

Various attempts have been made to study the correlation of gender assignments among the Romance languages. Dulsey (1956) found the following correlations in a list of 61 cognates:

Portuguese and Spanish (74.5 percent)
Italian and Spanish (62.7 percent)
Italian and Portuguese (59.7 percent)
French and Portuguese (35.7 percent)
French and Spanish (31.0 percent)
French and Italian (23.3 percent)

What these figures mean for the learner is that if he is, say, Portuguese, and studying Spanish, he could be 74.5 percent of the time correct in getting the right gender of the Spanish word if he simply transferred the assignment from his own language. Such figures are meaningless if we do not consider the semantic groupings into which the gender assignments fall. Another interesting implication for the evaluating of learning errors comes to the fore if we consider, say, the Italian-speaking learner of Spanish as opposed to an

English-speaking learner. If the Italian says, incorrectly, *el sangre* 'the blood' for *la sangre*, it is probably because *sangue*, the counterpart to *sangre* in his language, is masculine. On the other hand, if the English-speaking student says *el sangre*, it is most likely because he guessed at it, since English does not mark its nouns as to grammatical gender. If this notion is correct, the kinds of errors regarding gender which the Italian learner makes, will follow a pattern traceable to the situation in Italian while errors made by the English speaker will be random, in so far as [−animate] nouns are concerned.

Many languages, whether they have inflectional gender or not, contain words which refer to humans only, but do not specify sex. Some of these words in English are: *person, client, victim.* They are also 'sexless' in languages with gender, but are nevertheless assigned a surface gender:

Italian:	persona	'person' (feminine)
	vittima	'victim' (feminine)
German:	die Person	'person' (feminine)
	das Opfer	'victim' (neuter)

Some languages without inflectional gender do not associate the [male] and [female] opposition unless the situation somehow requires a clear distinction. Indonesian, for example, has a word *orang* which translates more or less as 'person' and is used to refer to both men and women in most situations. If a distinction akin to English 'man' and 'woman' is required, an appropriate modifier is added:

orang laki-laki	'man'
orang perempuan	'woman'

The same rule is in effect for animal names, but with [−human] modifier:

ajam	'fowl'
ajam djantan	'rooster'
ajam betina	'hen'

Much more could be said about how gender structures the lexicon of a language and how it can be called an inflectional category. We shall, however, drop the matter here to pass on to a consideration of how semantic features can be associated with pronouns. One final word of advice to the teacher who must be involved with inflectional gender: look for the patterns which the language establishes in associating semantic features with surface markers. There is apt to be a number of them, such as the 'fruit' and 'tree' set of the Romance languages. It is hardly of use to tell the student that the assignment of gender is totally arbitrary.

6.4 The Semantic Specification of Pronouns

The ways in which language is enmeshed in human society are amply illustrated by an analysis of the semantic features underlying pronouns. Depending on the particular language under investigation, one might find it necessary to characterize pronouns as expressing 'person,' 'number,' 'sex,' and so on. 'Person,' for example, cannot be explained unless we have recourse to communicational roles. 'First' person (I person) means reference to 'speaker,' 'second' person (II person) to 'addressee,' 'third' person (III person) to 'individual other than speaker or addressee.' 'Third' person is often extended to include nonhumans or inanimates. Thus, we have in English: *I* (I person), *you* (II person, singular or plural), and *he* or *she* or *it* (III person, including humans and nonhumans, animates, and inanimates). The pronoun *we* in English represents the speaker with (1) one or more addressees, or (2) one or more third persons, or (3) any number of addressees and other persons. The pronoun *they* is a plural of 'third person.' To characterize I, II, and III persons semantically in English, we might propose the following:

I person: [+human, α male, $-\alpha$ female, $-$number, +speaker]

II person: [+human, α male, $-\alpha$ female, $\pm$number, +addressee]

III person: [+human, α male, $-\alpha$ female, $\pm$number, +other]

(The symbols α and $-\alpha$ stand for alternative coefficients, [+male, $-$female, [$-$male, +female]; that is, when one feature is specified as +, the other is $-$, and vice versa. This convention is often used in phonological analysis, as in Chapter 7, where the use of α without the minus sign marks features having the same coefficients. We have decided to recognize [male] and [female] as different features rather than specifying [+female] as [$-$male]. The reason for this decision is because [$-$male] alone would not distinguish between 'neutered' males, like *ox, capon, eunuch* as a group and females. Also [+male, +female] is needed in order to discuss bisexual plants and animals.) Third person could also entail specifications like [inanimate] and [nonhuman].

For purposes of simplification in the contrastive procedure, we will refer to [I, II, III person] only in terms of 'speaker' or 'addressee' or 'other.' To the relatively simple semantic structure of pronouns in English, we can contrast that of Bengali, which specifies in various combinations: I, II, III person, number, honorifics, proximity to speaker, and human vs. nonhuman. The Bengali pronouns with the smallest number of specifications are those marked with [I person], where only number is variable:

ami   [I person]   amra   [I person]
      [−number]   [+ number]

II person specification allows reference to honorifics and proximity to speaker, in addition to number:

apni   [II person]   tumi   [II person]   tui   [II person]
       [+ honorific]   [−honorific]   [−honorific]
       [−number]   [−number]   [−number]
                                                          [+ proximal]

The [+number] counterparts to *apni, tumi,* and *tui* are, respectively, *apnara, tomra,* and *tora.*

The greatest degree of specification is found with the III person forms, where [±human], [±honoric], and [±proximal] are all operative in some way. They have been arranged in Table 6.3.

Table 6.3   Specifications of features for III person in Bengali

	ini	uni	tini	ẽra	õra	tãra	e	o	še	era
human	+	+	+	+	+	+	+	+	+	+
honorific	+	+	+	+	+	+	−	−	−	−
number	−	−	−	+	+	+	−	−	−	+
proximal	+	−		+	−		+	−		+

	ora	tara	eta	ota	šeta	egulo	ogulo	šegulo
human	+	+	−	−	−	−	−	−
honorific	−	−						
number	+	+	−	−	−	+	+	+
proximal	−		+	−		+	−	

Since honorifics do not function with nonhuman referents, no coefficient is specified. Notice also that the forms *tini, tãra, še, tara, šeta,* and *šegulo* do not specify proximity to speaker, while the others indicate nearness or distance.

The specification of honorifics in some languages can be associated with I person, as well as with II and III person. In Korean jə–num is used by the speaker to refer to himself when he is talking to persons higher in social position or older than he; [na-num] is used in speaking to friends, to those of the same age or younger, and to those who are of lower status.

If we wish to contrast two languages with regard to the semantic composition of their pronouns, we might find it useful to proceed in terms of how each language groups discrete features. It is also important to remember that such features, even if they do not constitute a particular pronoun, can be associated with some other surface form. English, for example, does not specify [honorific] in its pronouns, but there are other devices for indicating familiarity (cf. expressions like 'being on a first name basis') or nonfamiliarity (use of *Mr., Mrs., Miss* with the last name). While the existence of a particular surface form for honorifics (or, for that matter, for any semantic feature) would indicate that the speakers of the language place some importance on social standing, one should not assume that the lack of a surface form means the opposite. In short, the grammar of a language must always be presented in its sociocultural matrix.

6.5 Surface Derivation

In a very important way, every language is in a constant state of creation. Using its own surface patterns, it builds new groups of semantic features into lexemes. When the first astronauts were able to reach the moon, the Italians could talk of an *allunaggio*, a moon landing, on the model of *atterraggio*, an earth landing. A new verb could be formed: *allunare* 'to land on the moon,' on the model of *atterrare* 'to land on the earth.' In English one can now speak of a *moonscape* just as one has spoken of *landscapes* in the past.

Noticing the process of lexical interrelationship has led the grammarian to talk of *derivation*: nouns are said to be derived from other nouns, verbs from nouns, nouns from verbs, adjectives from nouns, and so on. Some patterns are obvious: *relate, relation, relational; organize, organization, organizational,* etc. Others are probably no longer active: *fox, vixen,* or *cat, kitten.* It is in view of the fact that derivational patterns, like inflectional ones, can become obsolete that the contrastive process best concentrates on those which are still productive. It is most unlikely, for example, that present-day speakers of English think of the word *orchard* as consisting of *hort* (garden) and *yard* and belonging to the set which includes *lumberyard, front yard, backyard,* and *Harvard Yard* (we might even include *vineyard,* despite its different stress pattern). Only one interested in the history of English might associate the stem *vir-* of *virile, virility* with the *wer-* of *werwolf,* which have the same Indo-European origins if one goes back far enough. Although to a lesser extent than inflection, derivation relies on pervasiveness of pattern in order to be recognized. It may well be that the only difference between 'inflection' and 'derivation' is one of degree of pervasiveness. The more frequent the pattern, the more inflectional it is, the less frequent, the more derivational it is. Adverb formation in -ly stands somewhere in the middle and subsequently leads to disagreement about its status among those linguists who concern themselves strictly with surface patterns.

We shall not go into a detailed discussion of surface arrangements and how they can differ from language to language. Instead, we turn to a matter involving derivation which is seldom treated. Each language follows its own patterns of lexicon structuring with regard to semantic composition. In contrasting languages, we often note that the very same (or almost identical) sets of semantic features are built into different parts of speech. The English traffic sign, *No Parking,* has as its German counterpart a noun: *Parkverbot.* One *plays* both *golf* and *tennis* in English but only *golf* is also a verb: *He golfs* and *He plays golf.* In French *golf* is only a noun: *Il fait du golf,* as is *tennis: Il joue au tennis.* Notice however that a different verb construction is used for *golf* and *tennis* in French. The semantic features underlying the verbal expression in English, *to pass a car,* i.e., while driving, are made either a noun or a verb in Italian: *sorpassare* (verb) and *sorpasso* (noun). German also has both a noun and a verb in this particular semantic field but the noun is apparently restricted to adverbial expressions: *beim Überholen,* i.e., 'while passing,' for example. Since such matters are not well understood, we have no formal procedure to suggest for contrasting the ways in which languages make their semantic groupings. At the moment, it seems that such processes are without patterning. The only recourse in language teaching is to label them special expressions or *idioms* whenever they differ from those of the student's native language. Doing so, however, is tantamount to sidetracking an important aspect of surface patterning and making a stable definition of *idiom* impossible.

6.6 Idioms

A discussion of idioms inevitably comes up with regard to language analysis and teaching. If we say: idioms exist only in contrasting one language with another, then we cannot describe the difference between expressions like *on the right foot* and *in a proper and correct manner* as involving idiomaticity, as in:

1. The professor started the course off on the right foot.
2. The professor began the course in a proper and correct manner.

Since native speakers would recognize that such expressions share semantic features, the problem is one of how to account for the overt differences. Some theorists would suggest a 'literalization' rule (see W. L. Chafe, 1967) to convert one of the set (taken as the idiom) into its literal counterpart. This procedure requires, of course, that we are always able to distinguish idioms from non-idioms, with the latter always being literal.

Following the lead of Chafe, we might consider idiomatization as a process whereby the semantic features that compose a lexeme are rearranged in hierarchical importance. Thus, underlying the lexeme *on the right foot* are semantic features referring to its original context (marching, dancing, etc. where using the right foot first is the proper way). If [+proper] is a feature underlying *on the right foot*, our idiom-making process would have it advanced to a position where the other features concerned with marching and dancing are subsequent to it. In other words, [+proper] becomes a central feature of meaning, where it once was peripheral. The process is not unlike that of metaphor, the only difference presumably being that in metaphor, previously unassociated semantic features are associated. With such an interpretation of idiom, or, better *idiomatization*, we can understand how one might claim that idioms exist only in cross-language comparison. A student is not likely to notice that *tener años* is an idiom in Spanish meaning *to be X years of age* if he speaks a language with a comparable expression, such as Italian *aver anni*. If, on the other hand, he does not, then he must associate the underlying semantics of *tener años* with those underlying the comparable expression in his language. In finding that he must advance in hierarchical importance some features of a lower or peripheral status in the semantics of his own language, he is performing a function not unlike that of Chafe's literalization or our advancement. Simply put, *tener años* comes to stand in the same relationship semantically to *have x years of age* as does *start off on the right foot* to *begin in a proper and correct manner*.

In this chapter we have only touched upon the many ways in which languages may build lexicons. Semantics is still a very unsettled study. Our intention was simply to show the guidelines for semantic study as related to language teaching. The only way in which our theoretical constructs will lose their provisional status is by intensive application.

6.7 Problems

1. Characterize each of the following in terms of shared and non-shared semantic features. If you are not certain about their meanings, look them up in a good English dictionary (data from Lamb, 1964).

cattle	horse	sheep	swine
cow	mare	ewe	sow
bull	stallion	ram	boar
steer	gelding	wether	barrow
heifer	filly	lamb	gilt
calf	colt		shoat
	foal		piglet

Hint: The following features should be included in your matrices: [male, female, neutered male,] and [mature/immature/adolescent].

2. The following represent a grouping of semantic features not found in English. Postulate the feature or set of features which English uses to differentiate each. Make a contrastive statement. Do you know of other languages which underdifferentiate terms referring to parts of the human body?

1. cos	(Irish)	leg, foot
2. nogá	(Russian)	leg, foot
3. ruká	(Russian)	arm, hand
4. dedo	(Spanish)	finger, toe
5. kidole	(Swahili)	finger, toe

3. Using a good bilingual dictionary, look up the meanings of each of the following and contrast them with their English counterparts:
    1. Spanish: esquina/rincon; saber/conocer
    2. French: belle/sympathique

4. Using a good dictionary and/or your own intuition as a speaker of English, prepare a feature matrix with appropriate plus/minus coefficients for the following pairs of words. Then contrast them with arrangements in another language of your choice.

1. kill/die	6. sell/buy
2. teach/learn	7. rob/steal
3. make/do (full verb)	8. loan/borrow
4. sensible/sensitive	9. send/receive
5. know/understand	10. like/please

5. The following words in English and French have been arranged in sets according to generally shared features. They are different in some important ways. Explain these differences in terms of postulated features, e.g.,

English   French
face   face
(feature not shared: reference to part of human anatomy. English [+anat. ref.] , French [−anat. ref.])

English   French
1. arm   arme
2. bank   banque
3. chance   chance
4. country   campagne
5. cry   crier
6. human   humain
7. large   large

If a dictionary does not help you in establishing the features for either language, you may wish to consult a native informant.

6. What semantic features are shared by the following lexemes in English:

> spyglass
> (eye)glasses
> monocle
> binoculars
> telescope
> microscope

Which of them has been named according to (a) field of vision, (b) organ of vision, (c) substance from which made, or (d) combinations of a, b, and c? Contrast your findings with another language.

7. Find translational equivalences in another language to the following English expressions:

charge a battery
charge a purchase (on your account)
charge a police barricade
load a gun
load the dice
load the merchandise (on a truck)

Is the same verb used to translate both *charge* and *load*? Does the other language make more than the two-way contrast of English? In what ways are *charge* and *load* semantically differentiated in English? How are the equivalents differentiated in the other language?

8. The following terms are used for grouping in English, e.g., *school* in *school of fish, pride* in *pride of lions*. Find equivalents in another language and postulate the kinds of semantic associations they entail (for example, *bovine, domesticated, equine*):

drove, herd, troop, yoke, span, flock, brace, swarm.

6.8 Notes

1. In our interpretation of semantics, features of meaning and their arrangements as lexemes are considered independently of their characterization in sound features and even their syntactic functions. Thus, the lexemes *brother* and *sister* share many features of meaning (common parentage, human, etc.) even though the words do not sound very much alike (cf. Spanish *hermano* and *hermana*). It might be helpful for the reader to think in terms of the Saussurean distinction *signifié* and *signifiant*, with the emphasis in this chapter on the *signifié* of words. A diachronic study involving the reassociation of semantic features in the lexemes of related languages is certainly feasible. A good example of such a study is Coseriu (1964).

2. There are many problems to be solved in applying feature analysis to semantics. It is often difficult to determine when the postulated feature represents one segment of meaning and when it is a composite of several. Moreover, theorists are not decided that feature analysis is the best way to handle semantics. We chose to proceed in terms of semantic features because such an analysis seemed sufficiently flexible in contrasting languages and also enforced the symmetry of our model of language design.

3. Anthropologists have, for some time, been interested in discovering the universal semantic features of human language. Casagrande (1963) refers to the need of all cultures to express the distinction between self and other persons and to provide for a spatiotemporal orientation. Slobin (1967) has an extensive bibliography on the subject of semantic fields, including kinship, social relations, color, time, and diseases.

4. Langendoen (1969; p. 37ff.) underlines the importance of remembering that semantic features derive not from properties of the physical world but are instead the results of the human mind and perceptual apparatus. The concept of warmth, for example, depends more on human perception than it does on any particular degree of temperature.

6.9 Background Readings

1. For a general discussion of features in semantic analysis:

Greenberg 1967
Leach 1970
Bolinger 1965
Bar-Hillel 1969
2. On application of feature analysis:
Lehrer 1969
Bjerke 1969
3. On metaphor:
Bickerton 1969
4. On the universality of color terms:
Berlin & Kay 1970
5. For a theoretical discussion of antonymy, synonymy and similar phenomena of meaning:
Lyons 1963

Chapter 7

THE PHONOLOGICAL

COMPONENT

In a very important way, all that we have said so far in this book about the design of human languages and the differences between languages is a prologue to this chapter on phonology. The phonological component deals with speech sounds which, in turn, are the only tangible manifestations of human language. The transitory turbulences in the air caused by the speaker as sound and heard by the listener in communication are the only 'realities' on which linguistic science can base its theories. Such theories are worthless if they cannot explain in some way how the production of speech sounds is connected to an underlying network of semantic and syntactic elements shared by speaker and listener.

The success of the listener in relating the sounds he hears to underlying elements of grammar is particularly impressive when we realize that man as a producer of sounds is far from perfect. Acoustical measurements via laboratory equipment reveal that no two speech sounds are ever exactly alike. Just how two different sounds can mean the same thing to a listener has led investigators to theorize that the phonological structure of a language must contain a basic stock of features which can be understood as present or absent in the production of a given sound. In this way, we can think of the sound which we symbolize as [n] as being *voiced, continuant, nasal,* and so on. Because we are interested here in whether or not such features are present in the production of a sound, we do not concern ourselves directly with the problem of explicating the physical and acoustic correlates to each feature. Suffice it to say that each sound feature represents an instruction to the speech mechanism, e.g., [+voice] means 'vibrate the vocal chords'; [+nasal], 'let air pass through nasal passage' and so on.

In surveying past work done in phonology, the reader will observe that such features of sound have been described either acoustically (e.g., compact, diffuse) or with reference to articulatory functions (e.g., rounding, dental, labial). (See the work of Jakobson and Halle 1956, for acoustics and Hockett 1955, for articulatory reference.) Since the usual situation among foreign language teachers is that they have no access to mechanical devices with which to measure and analyze sound, articulatory references have perhaps the greatest mnemonic value. Traditional descriptions of sounds for language teachers have most often employed articulation as their basis with, of course, varying degrees of success. The recent efforts of Harms (1968) and Chomsky & Halle (1968) to discuss phonological features represent a welcome drift away from reliance on instruments and toward the older tradition of articulation. The new classification, however, has a much greater degree of precision and structure than the older one.

It has been assumed that the production of speech sounds is primarily sequential and therefore analyzable in terms of discrete features. We observe, nevertheless, that some features appear to stretch over several sound units or accompany them in some way. Tone, for example, may accompany several syllables and be understood as rising, falling, level, and so on. Stress seems to have an affinity for vowels, and length can occur with either vowels or consonants. In the American tradition of phonological analysis, such features have been called *suprasegmentals*, while in the European schools, they are often referred to as *prosodics*.

We also observe that the arrangement of features in sound production may also be affected by the environment of a particular segment. As a result, we can speak of general patterns of sound arrangement such as the syllable, the phonological phrase or the utterance. Some linguists talk of *word level phonology* (see Chomsky & Halle, 1968) in order to distinguish between the sound characterization of stems and affixes and that of the syllable or of the utterance in general. Of crucial importance in determining the various groupings of sounds in a language is the notion of *juncture* or, in other words, the concatenation of sounds. As we shall see, particular languages can reveal a wide variety of junctural phenomena.

7.1 The Universal Stock of Features

As we did in our discussion of semantics, we propose a universal stock of features from which to derive the sound complexes of particular languages. Although the total range of features is unknown, linguists have had greater success in theorizing about phonological primes than they have had in the semantic area. This is because the mechanisms that produce and perceive speech sounds can be measured with instruments while semantics has to be inferred. Moreover, man's anatomy appears to limit the number of sounds he can produce and perceive to a far greater extent than it does his conception of semantic fields. It has even been possible to classify sound features into six major types with regard to the articulations associated with them, the acoustic impressions they make and the ways in which they pattern:

1. general or syllabicity-type features, such as *consonantal* (cns) or *vocalic* (voc), having to do with the patterning of sound;

2. oral-articulator features, such as *high* and *low*, referring to the up-and-down positioning of the tongue;

3. qualifying features, such as *retracted articulator* (retrac) or *proximal* (prox), with reference to the back and forward movement of the tongue;

4. manner features, such as *continuant* (cnt) or *abrupt offset* (abrof), referring to the ways in which the articulators move;

5. nonoral-articulator features, e.g., *voiced* (vce) or *nasal*, i.e., sounds arising outside the mouth (in the throat or nasal cavity);

6. prosodic features, e.g., *stress, tone*, i.e., features having to do with pitch, loudness, etc.

Several linguists have made claims about the universality of certain features (see, for example, Ladefoged, 1965) and the manner of discussing them is, at present, drifting toward the Jakobsonian-Praguian distinctive feature approach. Chomsky and Halle (1968), for example, distinguish between phonological features and phonetic ones. The former are binary and specifiable in terms of coefficients: + means distinctive presence and −, distinctive absence. Irrelevance or non-pertinence of a feature is either marked with O, or left unspecified. The latter type are absolutes in so far as they may be physically present in different ways independently of how they are perceived. Thus the phonetic feature [nasal] might be present in the production of a vowel but may or may not be perceived as distinctive by the hearer. In this book, we are centrally interested in phonological features, that is, features which are distinctive in speech, and therefore specifiable as absent or present. Several sources may be consulted as to the phonetic values of the features referred to in this book: Harms (1968), Chomsky & Halle (1968), McCawley (1967). Some readers may even find it useful to study anatomical descriptions of the vocal tract in order to better understand the production of sound. With the wealth of such material available, we shall forego any discussion of phonetic values either in acoustic or in articulatory terms. The features themselves will be, for the most part, suggestive of the phonetic values which they represent, e.g., [voiced], [nasal], [continuant] and so on.

7.2 Primary (Universal) Selection Rules

The primary selection rules, operating on the universal stock of phonetic features, must be general enough to account for the basic associations of features in all of human language. A main outcome of the primary selection rules is a general hierarchical ordering of features in a prototypical matrix. Thus, [consonantal] and [vocalic] are placed at the top of the hierarchy because it appears that they represent a basic distinction, without which all other discussion of sound features would be incomplete. Some would replace [vocalic] with [syllabic], as an even more basic feature (see Harms, 1968). The possibility exists of languages with no vowels, such as Kabardian, a Caucasian language (see Kuipers, 1970). In such cases, [syllabic] would include [vocalic] since one would need such a feature to refer to the syllabic nature of certain consonants in the language which may or may not include some phonetic vocalic coloring. Even in languages with vowels, one may encounter syllables where a consonant functions as a vowel: Serbo-Croatian [prst] 'finger,' [trst] 'Trieste' where [r] is syllabic. Whatever the case may be, a primary selection rule would be statable in the following terms:
To [vocalic] (or [syllabic]) associate [consonantal].
It is also of interest to note that no languages have been found yet which do not have some consonants. Moreover, it seems that in most languages, the number of consonants is greater than that of vowels. There may well be some anatomical and perceptive restraints which make it so.

The ordering of other features in our universal matrix is still to be determined. We can, however, make some useful speculations about which features are universally selected by languages. One of them would be [voicing]. It is difficult to envision a language which consists totally of voiceless sounds. Even if there were one, we would still have to posit at some stage, say, in the phonological redundancy rules, that all consonants and vowels in this language contain the feature [−voiced]. Chafe (1970) in his review of Postal's *Aspects of Phonological Theory* points out that a universal rule might exist to associate [rounded] with [back] in [+voc] segments.

It is certainly easier to speculate about what features are not universally selected by languages. They would include [aspiration], [palatalization], [length], and many others. When we say *not selected*, we mean that the feature or features in question do not figure in the description of sound complexes in a language. For example, some degree of aspiration must exist in all languages (if aspiration is associated with the expulsion of air), but it is definitely not relevant to the characterization of sounds in all languages. Laboratory studies suggest that the production of any sound is highly complex. Each language, however, centers on a limited number of features as critical to its own inventory. The output of the primary selection rules is a generally ordered set of features with no coefficients specified: [vocalic, consonantal, etc.]. It is the task of the secondary or specific selection rules to select some of the features as relevant and assign these features their coefficients.

Robert Harms (1968; p. 26) believes that the use of features to describe sounds cannot function on the basis of phonetic composition alone. He cites several cases from various languages in which useful generalizations about the patterning of features depends upon how such features are labeled. The sound [r] in Southern Paiute, for example, is best considered an obstruent, like [t]. It is our opinion that such problems are avoided when the phonological component is interpreted as having separate sets of universal and specific selection rules. The various groupings that Harms finds necessary are incorporated in the specific set of selection rules.

7.3 About Systematic and Autonomous Phonemes

The reader who is familiar with the type of phonological analysis done both by Europeans and Americans during the first part of the present century and continuing today, will note the conspicuous absence of any reference to the *phoneme*—a unit defined in various ways as the *smallest significant unit of sound in a language* or the *unit of sound capable of distinguishing meaning*, etc. It is important to realize that the phoneme is a descriptive device which is only as useful as the investigator wishes to make it. The notions of complementary distribution and free variation, to mention some, which underlie phonemics can be subsumed into a larger theory without involving the positing of phonemes. More importantly, the notion of phonemes based on the specifics of any language has been of little value in contrasting languages. We need to start from a level which is common, rather than try to contrast abstract units which do not derive from a common basis. Recently, some linguists have attempted to redefine the phoneme as a *systematic* unit of phonology—systematic in that it represents not only complexes of sound features but is also relatable to underlying syntax of a language. Thus, the former area of *morphophonemics* joins phonemics and one discusses variations in word shapes along with phonological units per se. Schane (1967) offers the following illustration of why explanations of phonological elements derive from underlying semantic and syntactic information but not vice versa. In French one says:

œ̃ savã ãglɛ

for *un savant anglais* meaning 'a scientist who is an Englishman' while

œ̃ savãt ãglɛ

(with liaison of [t]) means 'an Englishman who is a scientist.' Knowing when to make the liaison of the [t] requires semantic information. Since our goal is an explanation of how semantics and syntax are characterized as sound in particular languages, *any* symbol we might use is only a convenience, and nothing more. What we are attempting to do, is to explain how features of sound combine and change in the characterization of underlying grammatical elements. Thus, whatever symbol we choose to use at a given time represents various combinations of features. The symbol [N] may stand for all nasals in a language which assimilate to occlusive consonants ([−continuant]) which follow them:

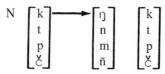

where N represents [+voice], [+nasal], [+continuant], but acquires all other features relevant to following consonants. At other times, it may prove convenient to use each individual symbol [ŋ n m ñ]. Such a distinction is especially important if we are comparing two languages, whose rules of assimilation differ in this respect. Stockwell & Bowen (1965; p. 14) provide some examples in contrasting English with Spanish.

7.4 Specific (Secondary) Selection Rules

It is in how particular languages utilize general features of sound that we can begin to discuss differences among them. Operating on the universal matrix of human sound production, each language displays some individuality in what features are chosen to function as prime differentiators of sound segments. We observe, for example, that while the vowels of French are on the whole more tense than those of Spanish, tenseness is ultimately not a distinctive feature for the vowels as a set in either language. Some of the ways in which specific matrices of sound features are built from universals can be illustrated if we take the following features with reference as to how vowels and semivowels are composed: [vocalic, consonantal, high, back, low, round, tense, voice]. If we were to describe a language that had only four vowels, say, [i], [u], [e], [a] (Hockett, 1955, reports such a situation for several, including Rutul, Apachean, some dialects of Nahuatl, and Shawnee) clearly the matrix in Table 7.1 is over-specified:

	[i]	[u]	[e]	[a]
voc	+	+	+	+
cns	−	−	−	−
high	+	+	−	−
back	−	+	−	+
low	−	−	−	+
round	−	+	−	±
tense	+	+	−	−
voice	+	+	+	+

Table 7.1
Over-specification
of Vowels

Assuming that our sample language also had full consonants (specifiable as [−voc, +cns]), semi-vowels ([−voc, −cns]), and liquids ([+voc, +cns]), we would have to keep the specification of [+ voc, −cns] for our vowels. We note however that if the coefficients of [high] are specified, [tense] is unneeded. The feature [round] is also redundant (even though [a] may be either rounded or unrounded). Since all vowels are [+ voice], this last feature is also redundant.

In spite of these redundancies, such an over-specified matrix is a necessary first step in phonological work because the absence or presence of a feature must first be specified before phonological redundancy rules can operate. Suppose, for example, that we were to contrast the above system with a language which had the same feature selection and even similar redundancies. It is altogether possible that such a language might mark [a] as only rounded ([+ round]) rather than optionally so (cf. Swedish). It might even allow the vowels to be optionally voiceless ([± voice]) instead of [+ voice]. Tenseness might turn out to be more important than [high] in representing the vowels—if various phonetic heights of vowels are allowed. As a result, the learner of such a language might find himself making errors of pronunciation even though his native language also contained the vowel set [i u e a]. The contrasts between the two sample languages may be stated in terms of the following selection rules:

1. For language A, select [±round] for [a];
    1a. For language B, select [+ round] for [a];
2. For language A, select [+ voice] for [+ voc, −cns];
    2a. For language B, select [±voice] for [+ voc, −cns], etc.

(Note that rules 2 and 2a are given in terms of features alone, since voicing is relevant to all vowels or segments marked [+voc, −cns]). It is evident that contrastive analyses which operate strictly in terms of phonemic units, be they autonomous or systematic, are hard put to discuss such *low-level* contrasts. Even though making a vowel [+ round] only, where the language to be learned marks it [±round] may not result in misunderstanding, it is, nonetheless, a difference. Redundancy may not be desired in a balanced system of description, but it does function at some point in the learning process and so must be incorporated into our CA.

Other examples of how features are selected and assigned different values can be found in a contrast of occlusive consonants among various languages. In Mandarin Chinese, [aspiration] functions to characterize different sets of occlusives, while [voicing] is optionally present in the unaspirated consonants:

	[p]	[t]	[c]	[k]	[p']	[t']	[c']	[k']
voice	±	±	±	±	−	−	−	−
aspr.	−	−	−	−	+	+	+	+

English, on the other hand, uses [voice] to separate [p t k] from [b d g], and assigns [aspiration] to the voiceless set under certain conditions: in syllable initial position, not preceded by [s], e.g.,

[p'ɪl] / [spɪl]

A segment of the English matrix would be:

	[p]	[t]	[k]	[b]	[d]	[g]
voice	−	−	−	+	+	+
aspr.	±	±	±	−	−	−

with subsequent phonological redundancy rules accounting for the two values of [aspiration] in different environments. The implications for the language learner are as follows: If he is English-speaking and learning Mandarin Chinese, he will most likely articulate segments like the following correctly: [p'a], since for him all voiceless initial occlusives are aspirated. He will also perceive [p'a] as a segment that is voiceless and aspirated. The segment [pa], on the other hand, may well be perceived as [ba]. If he, in turn, articulates [ba] for Mandarin Chinese [pa], it will most likely be perceived by the native speaker of Mandarin as [pa] since his English-like pronunciation of [ba] would not be aspirated. The difficulty comes when the learner learns enough Mandarin Chinese to realize that voiceless occlusives are not always aspirated. When this happens, he will begin to have difficulty with [pa], wondering whether he heard it as [p'a] or [pa]. The Chinese learner of English will tend to treat [voicing] in an offhand manner, pronouncing *bill* as either [bɪl] or [pɪl]. He would not have difficulty with words like *pill* since he would perceive the aspiration of [p'].

Modern Persian, to take another language, assigns [+ aspirated] to its voiceless stops and affricates regardless of whether or not they are preceded by [s]:

	[p]	[t]	[č̌]	[k]	[b]	[d]	[ǰ]	[g]
voice	−	−	−	−	+	+	+	+
aspir.	+	+	+	+	−	−	−	−

Thus the Persian-speaking learner of English will tend to say: [sp'ɪl] (or [isp'ɪl]) for English *spill*, as well as [p'ɪl] for *pill*. Conversely the English-speaking learner of Persian will tend not to aspirate occlusives after [s] in that language.

7.5 Phonological Redundancy Rules

If we were to construct fully specified matrices for each language under investigation, we would have something like that of Table 7.2 for Spanish, which covers only the main single segments in the language.

There are sound complexes which we have omitted, such as: [β δ γ ŋ] which would have to be included if we make any claim to comprehensiveness. Even with the segments we have characterized, it is evident that certain of the segments are over-specified and that some of the features in some of the segments are redundant. If, for example, we consider vowels ([+voc, −cns]) as a subset, we need only five features to describe them (Table 7.3). The other features become redundant and can be associated through a set of *phonological redundancy rules*. For example, we might posit the following rules to convey the information that all vowels specified as [+back, −low] in Spanish are also [+round] and those marked [−back, −low] are [−round]:

(1)   [+back] ⟶ [+round] / $\begin{bmatrix} +voc \\ -cns \\ -low \\ \underline{} \end{bmatrix}$

(2)   [−back] ⟶ [−round] / $\begin{bmatrix} +voc \\ -cns \\ -low \\ \underline{} \end{bmatrix}$

Table 7.2 Redundant matrix of Spanish segments

	i	u	e	o	a	y	w	R	r	l	λ	p	b	t	d	k	g	č	f	s	n	ñ	m	θ	x
voc	+	+	+	+	+	−	−	+	+	+	+	−	−	−	−	−	−	−	−	−	−	−	−	−	−
cns	−	−	−	−	−	−	−	+	+	+	+	+	+	+	+	+	+	+	+	+	+	+	+	+	+
high	+	+	−	−	−	+	+	−	−	−	−	−	−	−	−	+	+	+	−	−	−	+	−	−	+
back	−	+	−	+	+	−	+	−	−	−	−	−	−	−	−	+	+	−	−	−	−	−	−	−	+
low	−	−	−	−	+	−	−	−	−	−	−	−	−	−	−	−	−	−	−	−	−	−	−	−	−
ant.	−	−	−	−	−	−	−	+	+	+	+	+	+	+	+	−	−	−	+	+	+	−	+	+	−
coro.	−	−	−	−	−	−	−	+	+	+	+	−	−	+	+	−	−	+	−	+	+	+	−	+	−
round	−	+	−	+	−	−	+	−	−	−	−	−	−	−	−	−	−	−	−	−	−	−	−	−	−
tense	−	−	−	−	−	+	+	+	−	−	+	−	−	−	−	−	+	−	−	−	+	−	+	−	−
voice	+	+	+	+	+	+	+	+	+	+	+	−	+	−	+	−	+	−	−	−	+	+	+	−	−
cont.	+	+	+	+	+	+	+	−	−	+	+	−	−	−	−	−	−	−	+	+	+	+	+	+	+
nasal	−	−	−	−	−	−	−	−	−	−	−	−	−	−	−	−	−	−	−	−	+	+	+	−	−
strid.	−	−	−	−	−	−	−	−	−	−	−	−	−	−	−	−	−	+	+	+	−	−	−	+	+

(feature descriptions taken from Chomsky & Halle, 1968: ant. −anterior, coro. −coronal, cont. −continuant, strid. −strident).

Table 7.3 Specification of Spanish vowels

	i	u	e	o	a
voc	+	+	+	+	+
cns	−	−	−	−	−
high	+	+	−	−	−
back	−	+	−	+	+
low	−	−	−	−	+

Since [back] and [round] have the same coefficients, however, we can use the 'alpha' convention (α) to capture this fact in the form of a single rule:

$$(\text{la}) \quad [\, \alpha \text{ back}] \longrightarrow [\, \alpha \text{ round}] \, / \, \begin{bmatrix} +\text{voc} \\ -\text{cns} \\ -\text{low} \\ \underline{} \end{bmatrix}$$

In other words, where α equals '+' for [back], the coefficient of [round] is also '+', and where α is '−' for [back], it is also '−' for [round].

The use of only five features for Spanish is possible because it discriminates only five vowel segments. In Italian, however, the need would arise for the specification of an additional feature (e.g., [tense]) to accomodate the vowels [ɔ] and [ɛ] which stand in opposition to [o] and [e], respectively. Thus, we would mark [o] and [e] as [+tense] and [ɔ] and [ɛ] as [−tense].

Among the consonants we note that [low] does not serve to differentiate them from vowels, nor does [round]. Proceeding in this way, we obtain a set of redundancy rules and a non-redundant, language-specific matrix for each language involved in our CA. The non-redundant matrix for Spanish would look like the one in Table 7.4.

Table 7.4 Non-redundant matrix for Spanish sound segments

	i	u	e	o	a	y	w	R	r	l	λ	p	b	t	d	k	g	č	f	s	n	ñ	m	0	x
voc	+	+	+	+	+	−	−	+	+	+	+	−	−	−	−	−	−	−	−	−	−	−	−	−	−
cns	−	−	−	−	−	−	−	+	+	+	+	+	+	+	+	+	+	+	+	+	+	+	+	+	+
high	+	+	−	−	−	+	+	−	−	−	−	−	−	−	−	+	+	+	−	−	−	+	−	−	+
back	−	+	−	+	+	−	+	−	−	−	−	−	−	−	−	+	+	−	−	−	−	−	−	−	+
low	−	−	−	−	+																				
ant.								+	+	+	+	+	+	+	+	−	−	−	+	+	+	−	+	+	−
coro.								+	+	+	+	−	−	+	+	−	−	+	−	+	+	+	−	+	−
tense								+	+	+	−	−	+	−	−	−	−	+	−	−	−	+	−	+	−
voice												−	+	−	+	−	+								
cont.								−	−	+	+	−	−	−	−	−	−	+	+	+	+	+	+		+
nasal																		−	−	−	+	+	+		
strid.												−	−	−	−	−	−	+	+	+	−	−	−	+	+

Redundancy rules would specify that all segments marked [+voc, −cns], that is, vowels, are also [−ant., −coro.]. Also, all segments unspecified for [nasal] and [strident] are redundantly [−nasal] and [−strident], and all segments unmarked for [voice] are [+voice]. Voicing functions to distinguish segments only if they are [−voc, + cns, −cont.] , or, in other words, if they are stops.

Taking this last-mentioned feature, we can illustrate some basic points of contrast between languages. One of the differences between Spanish and English, for example, is that [voice] is not a redundant feature for strident consonants in English while it is in Spanish. The English set includes:

	č	ǰ	f	v	s	z
voice	−	+	−	+	−	+

As a result, the Spanish-speaking learner of English will have to accustom himself to using [voice] more pervasively than he does in his own language. In doing so, he is liable to make any number of different associations of features. A common one is associating the features of [v] with those of [b] , pronouncing 'berry' for both *berry* and *very*. There are, of course, several reasons for this phenomenon. In addition to the matter of voicing, Spanish also has a spirantalized ([+ continuant]) segment [β] which interacts with [b] in the characterization of morphemes (see below) which is similar enough to English [v] to reinforce the association. More will be said about such matters in the discussion on characterization rules, below. First, we shall illustrate some of the ways in which particular languages associate the same stock of features in different ways.

French associates [+ round] with both [+ back] and [−back] in its vowels and glides (Table 7.5)

Table 7.5 A partial matrix for French vowels and glides

	i	ü	u	y	ẅ	w
voc	+	+	+	−	−	−
cns	−	−	−	−	−	−
back	−	−	+	−	−	+
round	−	+	+	−	+	+

where [ü] and [ẅ] are [−back] and [+round], e.g., *lit, loue, lui, Louis, lu, lier*. The learner of French whose native language does not combine these features in this way is apt to make several kinds of errors. For one, he may simply ignore one of the features (either [backness] or [rounding]), pronouncing *lu* ([lü]) as either [li] or [lu] . If he says [li] then he merges *lu* with *lit*, if he says [lu] , he fails to distinguish between *loue* and *lu*, and so on. The learner may also separate the combined features into two vowel segments, saying [liu] for *lu*, etc. That this can happen is attested to by the modern pronunciation of words in English borrowed from French such as *view* [vyuw], from *vue*.

German also combines rounding with [−back] or front vowels. In addition, it associates a feature [tense] which is non-redundant (see Moulton, 1962). These features are arranged in Table 7.6.

Table 7.6 Feature specification for German vowels

	i̦	i	u̦	u	ü̦	ü	e̦	e	o̦	o	ö̦	ö	a̦	a
high	+	+	+	+	+	+	−	−	−	−	−	−	−	−
back	−	−	+	+	−	−	−	−	+	+	−	−	+	+
round	−	−	+	+	+	+	−	−	+	+	+	+	−	−
tense	+	−	+	−	+	−	+	−	+	−	+	−	+	−

(Tense vowels are also slightly longer than non-tense vowels.) The manner in which the features [high back round tense] are arranged hierarchically in the German vowel system can be illustrated in the form of a tree diagram (Figure 7.1). In contrast to French vowels which, on the whole, tend to be tense and Spanish vowels which are non-tense, the vowels of German are distinguished according to this feature. For this reason, both the French-speaking and the Spanish-speaking learner of German would have problems, with the French speaker tending to make all vowels tense and the Spanish speaker making them all non-tense. The Spanish speaker would have the additional problem of associating [+round] with [−back].

Turkish not only associates [+round] with [−back] vowels but also [−round] with [+back] to produce a symmetrical set of eight segments (Table 7.7).

Table 7.7 Specification of Turkish vowels

	i	ü	ɨ	u	e	ö	o	a
high	+	+	+	+	−	−	−	−
back	−	−	+	+	−	−	+	+
round	−	+	−	+	−	+	+	−

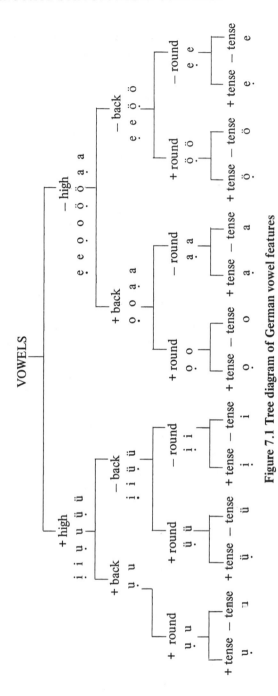

Figure 7.1 Tree diagram of German vowel features

The symmetry is especially evident if we arrange the vowel segments in the form of a box diagram (with the front side or lower side representing the feature [−back], the vertical dimension, [height] and the horizontal dimension [rounding]) (Figure 7.2).

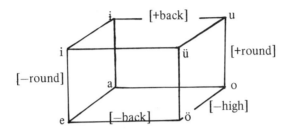

Figure 7.2 Box diagram for Turkish vowels

It is not just happenstance that such a system exists for Turkish since sets of features operate in what is called *vowel harmony* to restrict permissible sequences of vowels in words. The vowel of the plural marker *ler/lar* depends on the last vowel of the noun stem: *asker* 'soldier' becomes *askerler* 'soldiers' and *baba* 'father' becomes *babalar* 'fathers'. In other words, [−back] vowels are followed by [−back] vowels and [+back] vowels by [+back].

Much more can be said about the ways in which languages select features of sound and combine them in different ways. The preceding discussion should serve to give some insight into the kinds of matrices one would have to construct for languages and how redundancy rules would have to be written. We turn now to the final set of rules in the phonological component—those which characterize as strings of sound those bundles of semantic features which are tied together syntactically. For convenience, we shall utilize the well-known linguistic term *morpheme* to identify segments of semantic and syntactic data.

7.6 Phonological Characterization Rules

In order to characterize strings of morphemes as sound, it is convenient to consider the phonological rules as operating on units of different sizes. There are characterization rules which pertain to general morpheme shapes and sequences while others apply to smaller groupings. For example, we can observe that if a word in English is characterized as beginning with a segment [s] followed by a [−cont] consonant (or 'stop'), that stop is always voiceless ([−voice]): [sp st sk] as in *spill, still,* and *skill.* We also observe that in

Spanish no word can begin with a cluster like [sp st sk]. When speakers of Spanish attempt to learn English, they often pronounce words like *steam* and *state* with an initial vowel [e], making them indistinguishable from *esteem* and *estate*. Before going into detail with regard to characterization rules, we shall briefly discuss some general properties of phonology.

It has been customary to interpret the sounds of languages as being arranged in groupings of different sizes. The smallest (or briefest) grouping of sound segments that can be uttered by a speaker is called the *syllable*. Its structure differs from language to language but it can be considered to have a peak of prominence (see Hockett, 1955, for discussion of term) identifiable in many languages as a vocalic segment, with or without the accompaniment of consonantal segments ('true' consonants are those which are excluded from occurrence as peaks of prominence). Words can be thought of phonologically as well as grammatically. In their phonological sense, they are groupings of syllables which can be pronounced alone or in combination with other such units. In this way, 'word' overlaps with 'syllable' since words can consist of single syllables or combinations of them, e.g., English *might* (S), *mighty* (SS), *mightily* (SSS). If we look at the word in terms of its grammatical content, it can be shown that some morphemes are given independent word status (such as *might*) while others become parts of words (*-y* and *-ly* of *mighty* and *mightily*). It is precisely in the context of word-grouping that linguists have been led to define some morphemes as 'free' (i.e., with 'word status') and others as 'bound' (without 'word status'). Words interpreted as groupings of sound segments can be of great importance in understanding how some rules of characterization operate. In German, for example, all voiced consonants with the exception of glides and liquids are devoiced in word-final position. Thus the words *Rad* and *Rat* are both pronounced [ra:t] —regardless of whether or not the next word begins with a vowel. Russian allows consonant segments [gd] to initiate words: [gḍe] 'where', while English does not. Such clusters can be found in English, however, at the ends of words: [bægd] 'bagged'. The difference between word junctures and syllable junctures in English makes possible the audible difference between *night rate* and *nitrate* ([t+r] vs. [tr]). In languages like French, on the other hand, word junctures do not so affect the concatenation of sound segments, e.g., the same pronunciation for both *trois petits trous* '3 little holes' and *trois petites roues* '3 little wheels'.

It appears that all languages have, in some way, rules of characterization that depend on how sounds are concatenated. In Spanish, [b d g] lose their occlusiveness between vowels, e.g., *haber, ido, hago* with [β], [δ], and [γ], respectively. In terms of our matrix for Spanish sound segments, we could represent this fact as follows:

[−contunant]⟶[+continuant] / [+vocalic] _____ [+vocalic]

If a word boundary is present, the rule is not operational. In some dialects of Spanish, word boundaries operate to affect rearrangements of sound features. Nasals occurring at the ends of words in such dialects must have the features [+high, +back, −coronal], symbolized as [ŋ]. Because of this fact, the Spanish-speaking learner of a language which has word-final nasals such as [n ñ m ŋ] will tend to articulate them all as [ŋ]. An inspection of the feature matrix for each nasal shows how they are distinct:

	n	ñ	m	ŋ
high	−	+	−	+
back	−	−	−	+
coron.	+	+	−	−

Using the symbol # to stand for word boundary, we can state the Spanish speaker's interpretation of word-final nasals in terms of the following rule:

$$[\text{+nasal}] \longrightarrow \begin{bmatrix} \text{+high} \\ \text{+back} \\ -\text{coronal} \end{bmatrix} / \underline{\hspace{1cm}} \#$$

Other rules would be needed in Spanish to cover the restrictions on feature arrangement within word boundaries, from syllable to syllable, e.g., the assimilation of nasals to occlusives resulting in [mp nt ñč ŋk, etc.].

Phonological characterization would be quite simple if it operated solely in terms of general groupings like syllable and word. If such were the case, the only requirement would be to associate one set of phonological features to each morpheme and discuss the general rules of arranging them in strings. Unfortunately, no language is known where phonological characterization is so limited. Such a language would have no variation in sound representation of its morphemes. Not only do languages display variation in sound/morpheme association, but they also impose a range of different restrictions on them. Take the matter of pluralization in English. There is a highly recurrent pattern in which [PLU] (pluralization) is characterized by a $\begin{bmatrix} \text{+coronal} \\ \text{+strident} \end{bmatrix}$ consonant:

1. [s], as in *lips, hats, sacks*
2. [z], as in *bags, fads, ribs*

An observation is that the voicing of the strident consonant representing plurality is predictable in terms of the final sound of the noun stem, thus it is voiced after a voiced sound and voiceless after a voiceless one. We might even suppose that this pattern of voicing is in accordance with a general phonological rule in English which disallows any other combination of coronal stridents with other sounds in word-final position. Even if we could not formulate such a rule, we could still restrict it to the characterization of [PLU] in the following way:

$$PLU \longrightarrow \begin{bmatrix} +\text{continuant} \\ \alpha\text{voice} \\ +\text{coronal} \\ +\text{strident} \end{bmatrix} \bigg/ \;[_N \ldots \alpha\text{voice}]_N \text{———} \#$$

That is to say, the characterization of [PLU] is [−voice] when the noun stem terminates in a [−voice] segment and is [+voice] if the noun stem has a final [+voice]. We then notice that English also contains plurals like the following with [əz]: *bushes*, *roses*, *matches*, which leads us to add a rule of linear restriction that if [PLU] contains $\begin{bmatrix} +\text{coronal} \\ +\text{strident} \end{bmatrix}$ and is preceded by a noun also with $\begin{bmatrix} +\text{coronal} \\ +\text{strident} \end{bmatrix}$ in its terminal segment, a vocalic segment must be inserted. The rule could be written as follows:

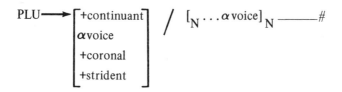

$$PLU \longrightarrow \begin{bmatrix} +\text{voc} \\ -\text{cns} \\ -\text{high} \\ +\text{back} \\ -\text{low} \\ -\text{round} \end{bmatrix} \begin{bmatrix} +\text{continuant} \\ +\text{voice} \\ +\text{coronal} \\ +\text{strident} \end{bmatrix} \bigg/ \begin{bmatrix} \ldots +\text{coronal} \\ _N \quad +\text{strident} \end{bmatrix}_N \text{———} \#$$

$$(\text{ə}) \qquad\qquad (\text{z}) \qquad\qquad (\check{\text{c}}, \check{\text{s}}, \text{s}, \text{z}, \text{etc.})$$

Up to this point, we can discuss [PLU] in its various forms with reference to the phonological composition of the noun with which it occurs. Even variations like *knife* and *knives*, *wife* and *wives*, can be accounted for in terms of variations in feature composition—this time of the noun itself, where the [voice] feature of the final segment of the noun is given the value

[+voice] when occuring with PLU and [−voice] otherwise. Incidentally, the [voice] feature also serves in a surface derivation, relating nouns and verbs as in:

use ([−voice], noun)   *use* ([+voice], verb)
house ([−voice], noun)   *house* ([+ voice], verb)

However, when we come to cases like *mouse* and *mice, foot* and *feet, child* and *children, ox* and *oxen, phenomenon* and *phenomena,* we must include in our rules of phonological characterization elements of semantics which specify each of these particular morphemes. This is tantamount to a rule of the type:

$$[_N \text{child}]_N + [\text{PLU}] \longrightarrow [_N \text{children}]_N$$

Fortunately, plurals with coronal stridents are far and away the most common in English and rules of this latter type would be few in number. As a matter of general observation, the phonological characterization rules of any language should proceed from the general to the specific in a way similar to those given above for English.

A great number of different phonological interpretations can be given pluralization in the languages of the world. At one extreme we find Chinese which specifies plural only by the use of a number morpheme (indefinite plural is not specified). Arabic has a different set of endings for various groupings: dual, paucal, many, etc. Italian has [PLU] semantically specified as in English, but instead, a vowel change is involved: *casa* 'house' and *case* 'houses.' Spanish has a plural with coronal stridents as English but with fewer rules of characterization than English:

$$(1)\ \text{PLU} \longrightarrow \begin{bmatrix} - & \text{high} \\ - & \text{back} \\ + & \text{anterior} \\ + & \text{coronal} \\ - & \text{tense} \\ + & \text{continuant} \\ + & \text{strident} \\ & (s) \end{bmatrix} \bigg/ \begin{bmatrix} + & \text{vocalic} \\ - & \text{consonantal} \\ & N \end{bmatrix}_N \underline{\qquad\qquad} \#$$

(a, o, e)

Such a rule accounts for: *señora* and *señoras; lobo* and *lobos, madre* and *madres,* etc. Another rule would be needed for sets like: *ciudad* and *ciudades; señor* and *señores:*

$$(2)\ \text{PLU} \longrightarrow \begin{bmatrix} + & \text{voc.} \\ - & \text{cns.} \\ - & \text{high} \\ - & \text{back} \end{bmatrix} \begin{bmatrix} - & \text{high} \\ - & \text{back} \\ + & \text{ant.} \\ + & \text{coro.} \\ - & \text{tense} \\ + & \text{cont.} \\ + & \text{strid.} \end{bmatrix} \Bigg/ \begin{bmatrix} + & \text{voc.} \\ \pm & \text{cns.} \\ & {}_N \end{bmatrix}_N \underline{\hspace{2cm}} \#$$

(e)

(s)

Although there are some general similarities of these two rules to those of English, the environments are quite different, the vowel of -es is different from that of English, and voicing does not figure in the Spanish rules. The kinds of errors that the Spanish-speaking learner of English will make are, perhaps, more obvious than those of the English-speaking learner of Spanish. One would expect the English speaker to interpret Spanish -es according to the English -es, pronouncing [əz], but it is even possible that he will apply his first rule (in an early stage of learning), producing [señorz] for *señores* or [θiudadz] for *ciudades.*

The foregoing discussion gives some idea of how phonological characterization rules operate in particular ways in particular languages. It is apparent that where some languages have complex steps, others do not. By investigating the different types of rules a language may have, the teacher of that language can determine the range of possible mispronunciation of his students. In this chapter, we have advanced the position that acquisition of pronunciation depends not only on general phonological properties but also on underlying morphemic structure—because the types of errors a learner can make, can derive from various points in the phonological component. If such a claim is correct, we can question instructional programs which proceed on the basis that pronunciation should be acquired before much of the underlying grammar is taught. At the very least, it appears that grammar and pronunciation are intimately connected and should be taught as such.

7.7 Problems

1. With reference to the matrix of features given below, the following words in English all share features:

1. seen
2. seam
3. sing
4. zing
5. thin
6. thing
7. theme

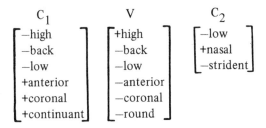

Questions:
   a. What are the unique features for each segment?
   b. What rules would need to be drawn up to explain
   what the Spanish-speaking learner of English would
   do in pronouncing them all identically as
   [siŋ]?

2. Column one, below, contains the written representations of how some speakers of Japanese mispronounce the English words given in column two. On the basis of these data, (a) make as many speculations as you can substantiate concerning the arrangement of consonants and the formation of the word in Japanese; (b) offer a prediction of how a Japanese might similarly 'mispronounce' the following: *slowly, still, ball, facts, brick, free, flee.*

I	II
gaaru furendo	girl friend
furuutsu	fruits
supiido	speed
sutairu	style
sekkusu	sex
miruku	milk
derakkusu	deluxe

3. The data given for Turkish and Indonesian (taken from Koutsoudas, 1966) illustrate two ways in which languages phonetically express the plural of noun stems:

Turkish:

1. diš 'tooth'	1a. dišler 'teeth'
2. çocuk 'child'	2a. çocuklar 'children'
3. asker 'soldier'	3a. askerler 'soldiers'
4. kedi 'cat'	4a. kediler 'cats'
5. masa 'table'	5a. masalar 'tables'
6. gece 'night'	6a. geceler 'nights'
7. baba 'father'	7a. babalar 'fathers'
8. kuš 'bird'	8a. kušlar 'birds'

Indonesian:

1. kursi 'chair'	1a. kursikursi 'chairs'
2. ibu 'mother'	2a. ibuibu 'mothers'
3. rumah 'house'	3a. rumahruman 'houses'
4. medzah 'table'	4a. medzahmedzah 'tables'
5. buku 'book'	5a. bukubuku 'books'

a. Formulate rules to explain each procedure.

b. What general statements can you make about the differences between the two procedures?

4.   Write general characterization rules for Italian and Rumanian regarding the definite article in each language and then prepare a set of contrastive statements for (1) Rumanian to Italian and (2) Italian to Rumanian.

A. Italian (in transcription):

1. [gátto] (masc.) 'cat'	1a. [ilgátto] 'the cat'
2. [amíko] (masc.) 'friend'	2a. [lamíko] 'the friend'
3. [šópero] (masc.) 'strike'	3a. [lošópero] 'the strike'
4. [spékkio] (masc.) 'mirror'	4a. [lospékkio] 'the mirror'
5. [libro] (masc.) 'book'	5a. [illíbro] 'the book'
6. [ánima] (fem.) 'soul'	6a. [lánima] 'the soul'
7. [siépe] (fem.) 'hedge'	7a. [lasiépe] 'the hedge'
8. [térra] (fem.) 'earth'	8a. [latérra] 'the earth'
9. [zbórnia] (fem.) 'drunkenness'	9a. [lazbórnia] 'the drunkeness'
10. [sféra] (fem.) 'sphere'	10a. [lasféra] 'the sphere'

11. [zbúffo] (masc.) 'puff'
12. [skálpo] (masc.) 'scalp'
13. [sistema] (masc.) 'system'

B. Rumanian (in transcription)
1. [óm] (masc.) 'man'
2. [óu] (masc.) 'egg'
3. [púi] (masc.) 'chicken'
4. [núme] (masc.) 'name'
5. [kărbúne] (masc.) 'coal'
6. [lúp] (masc.) 'wolf'
7. [kópil] (masc.) 'child'
8. [fátă] (fem.) 'girl'
9. [kárte] (fem.) 'book'
10. [moárte] (fem.) 'death'
11. [másă] (fem.) 'table'
12. [stéa] (fem.) 'star'
13. [básma] (fem.) 'kerchief'

11a. [lozbúffo] 'the puff'
12a. [loskálpo] 'the scalp'
13a. [ilsistéma] 'the system'

1a. [ómul] 'the man'
2a. [óul] 'the egg'
3a. [púiul] 'the chicken'
4a. [númele] 'the name'
5a. [kărbúnele] 'the coal'
6a. [lúpul] 'the wolf'
7a. [kópilul] 'the child'
8a. [fáta] 'the girl'
9a. [kártea] 'the book'
10a. [moártea] 'the death'
11a. [mása] 'the table'
12a. [stéaua] 'the star'
13a. [básmaua] 'the kerchief'

7.8 Notes

1. Experimentation continues on the acoustic correlates of human speech sounds. There is some question that the features customarily used to identify sounds are entirely accurate or appropriate. We have, nevertheless, adopted the features as proposed by Chomsky & Halle (1968). The reader may wish to consult Lisker & Abramson (1964) for an idea of some of the experimentation being conducted on sound composition. For extensive work on the surface phonetic patterning of various languages, see Delattre (1963) and Delattre & Olsen (1969). The latter study provides much useful information about syllabification in English, German, French, and Spanish, thereby alerting the teacher to possible learning problems in timing.

2. Saltarelli (1970) observes the similarities of plural inflection in Spanish and English and proposes a number of rules for Spanish. He also associates Spanish -es (as a plural) with es- at the beginnings of words, e.g., espalda, escuela, as being part of the same phenomenon.

3. Wardhaugh (1967) outlines various approaches to contrasting the phonologies of different languages. The reader may wish to compare his

remarks about the application of generative rules with the discussion in this chapter.

7.9 Background Readings

1. For an understanding of how this chapter has been organized:
   Harms 1968
   Chomsky & Halle 1968
2. For a contrastive study of the sounds of French and Italian:
   Companys 1965
3. On phonic interference:
   Ritchie 1968
4. On contrastive phonetics:
   Delattre & Olsen 1969. The study by Delattre and Olsen is primarily one of statistics. It reports on the ratio of consonants to vowels in the languages under investigation. While such frequency studies are interesting, their relevance to CA is questionable. They may, however, be of use in the grading and organization of teaching materials.

5. For the CA of English with other languages:
   Moulton 1962
   Stockwell & Bowen 1965
   Agard & Di Pietro 1965
6. For a good survey of the application of distinctive feature analysis to various languages: Muljačić 1969.

Chapter 8

CONTRASTIVE ANALYSIS

AND THE

FOREIGN LANGUAGE TEACHER

In his theory of instruction, Bruner (1966) places great importance on what he calls *competence drive*. It is this competence drive or *instinct for workmanship*, as Thorstein Veblen termed it (quoted in Bruner, 1966) that leads humans to excel in some tasks. The interest shown by the student in the program of instruction is at least as important as the content of the program. As Bruner sees it, the teacher must sustain or, better, build the student's motivation to go on through successive learning tasks. No degree of structuring in the program can compensate for a lack of interest on the part of the student for what is being taught. Following Bruner's lead, we can view all programs of foreign language instruction from two perspectives: (1) the model of language competence they purport to build and (2) the devices they employ to promote competence drive, whereby learning is made possible.

The model of language design which we have presented in this book, with its three interlocking components of rules, should be understood as an effort to provide a general framework of competence. As such, it is subject to change or even rejection, should it be contradicted by some facts of performance. We have, however, found it useful in providing for an explanation of language in both its universal and particular aspects. It should also be clear to the reader by now that the new language competence that we as teachers would like to create in our students consists basically of those elements of the target language which are different from those of the native language. There is support for this view of second language competence from both linguistics and psychology. Application of a simplicity metric to our interpretation of second language competence leads us to formulate rules which are neither universal nor particular to the grammar of the native language. To repeat universals or shared language-specific rules in our model of the competence to be acquired is linguistically superfluous. If transfer and interference are psychologically valid notions, many errors committed by the language learner can be traced back to precisely this matter of applying language-specific rules which are *not* found in the target language. Therefore, if the simplicity metric is correctly applied and if transfer does occur, the two notions complement one another in supporting CA as a valid endeavour in constructing pedagogically useful theories of second language competence. In fact, an inspection of textbooks written at various times in the past would lead us to suspect that CA has been performed intuitively in foreign language work. The treatment of gender, say, in a book of French for Spanish speakers is often quite different in terms of coverage and importance than it is in a book of French for speakers of English.

8.1 Pedagogical and Scientific Grammars

If by grammar we mean some sort of formalization of a model of competence, we must conclude that the differences between what are called *pedagogical* grammars on one hand and *scientific* grammars on the other, are theoretically trivial (for remarks on the matter see Del Olmo 1968, Bull 1965, and Saporta 1966). No doubt there are many differences to be found between the ways in which the teacher presents the grammar of the language he is teaching and the ways in which the linguist writes the rules of that grammar on a piece of paper; these differences, however, pertain to competence drive and not to the model of competence itself. That is to say, the explanations of how a language works, as given by a linguist, might be found to be irrelevant to a program of instruction in the language. They may not be very effective in motivating the student to speak the language. Nevertheless, the use of different pedagogical devices to impart the same knowledge of the language to the student cannot alter the facts of the language. Otherwise, the student would utter incorrect sentences. Whatever pedagogical devices the teacher may wish to employ, they are to be evaluated strictly in terms of how well they promote learning. There is no reason to assume that learning involves the recitation of grammatical rules. If and when the student uses the subjunctive correctly, we can say that he knows the rule for it. He may have acquired knowledge of the rule through any number of pedagogical devices. To decide whether or not the memorization of rules is appropriate to a program of language instruction is entirely independent of deciding whether or not the grammar of a language has been adequately covered in some way. As models of competence, we can compare pedagogical and scientific grammars only in so far as they are accurate, complete, explicit, and simple. To make what we have said here practical, it can be boiled down to advising the language teacher to examine the grammatical coverage of his instructional program independently of its presentation in order to determine the extent and accuracy of coverage. Any scientific grammar that he would have at his disposal would help him in serving as a point of reference in his survey. Once he decides that the coverage is accurate and adequate, he can turn to the matter of presentation itself.

8.2 Hierarchies of Difficulty

In 1950 Hans Wolff suggested a hierarchy of difficulty involving Puerto Ricans learning English. Others, such as Weinreich (1953) and Lado (1957) have also employed the concept. William Moulton (1962a) can be singled out in his attempt to provide a general framework for the use of contrastive data and the theory of transfer in deciding the relative importance of potential errors on the part of the learner. Stockwell and Bowen (1965) devote an entire chapter to the same matter, with special reference to Spanish for speakers of English. Characterizing the pronunciation of a language as a set of optional and obligatory operations which produce the appropriate sounds and sound sequences in that language, Stockwell and Bowen (1965, p.10) establish eight possible sets of contrasts:

Native Language Choice	Target Language Choice
1. Op(tional)	Op(tional)
2. Ob(ligatory)	Op
3. null	Op
4. Op	Ob(ligatory)
5. Ob	Ob
6. null	Ob
7. Op	null
8. Ob	null

A ninth possibility, null in both languages, is omitted for obvious reasons. To illustrate the types briefly, we might find that two features, x and y, are permissible in the same environment in both languages. They would be of type 1 (Op in both native and target languages). If feature x, but never y, is found in a given environment in the native language, and the choice remains optional in the target language, we would have a contrast of the second type (Ob in native, Op in target language). Once the eight types are identified with actual examples, they can be ranked in a hierarchy of difficulty, with the most difficult (from the learner's point of view) being the situation in which the target language has an obligatory choice and there is null in the native language and the least difficult, the situation of obligatory choices in both languages. Table 8.1 is an adaptation of the one Stockwell and Bowen provide their readers (p.16).

Table 8.1 Hierarchy of difficulty (after Stockwell & Bowen 1965)

Difficulty		Comparison		Type
Magnitude	Order	Native Lg.	Target Lg.	
I	1	null	Ob	6
	2	null	Op	3
	3	Op	Ob	4
II	4	Ob	Op	2
	5	Ob	null	8
	6	Op	null	7
III	7	Op	Op	1
	8	Ob	Ob	5

The following are paraphrases of the illustrations provided by Stockwell and Bowen (English as native language and Spanish as target) in descending order of difficulty:

1. Native language null, Target Language Ob: a sound segment [β] in Spanish with no counterpart in English.
2. Native language null, Target Language Op: Spanish with an opposition between [R] and [r], English with no such opposition.
3. Native Language Op, Target Language Ob: Spanish with variants [d] and [ð] of one phoneme class conditioned by environments, English with similar sound segments but without such restrictions.
4. Native Language Ob, Target Language Op: Spanish with a contrast of vowel height (high versus mid) before [n], e.g., *sino/seno*, some southern dialects of American English where there is variation, e.g., *pin/pen*.
5. Native Language Ob, Target Language null: English with a flap [r] replacing [t] in words like *photo, butter* and *patty,* Spanish with no such variation.
6. Native Language Op, Target Language null: English with a vowel [æ], Spanish with no such sound.
7. Native Language Op, Target Language Op: many words in both languages may have as their first sound segments a number of similar consonants like [p t k s m].
8. Native Language Ob, Target Language Ob: Both languages require that a vowel segment follow the cluster [sw] at the beginning of words.

Hierarchy of difficulty is not the only consideration of importance in the arranging of instructional materials. Stockwell and Bowen add functional load (i.e., the frequency with which the contrast in question comes up in actual speech), potential mishearing and pattern congruity (the reoccurrence of a specific feature in the system of the target language, e.g., aspiration accompanying a number of voiceless stops in English which may or may not be like the pattern of aspiration in the native language). If such hierarchies are to be applied in planning programs of instruction, it should be remembered that every speech act is a complex act, containing elements of semantics, syntax and phonology occurring simultaneously. Suppose, for example, that in the native language of a learner of English, all word-final consonants are devoiced. In addition, let us suppose that in this language, there is no derivational pattern comparable to the English one in which stems can fluctuate between noun and verb classes in the surface structure. If our learner of English mispronounces the verb *use* as [yuws] (the noun) instead of [yuwz], is it because of the phonological differences, the syntactical patterns or both? In view of the model of language design which we present in this book, it would seem that the seriousness of error-making is a function of the generality of the rule incorrectly transferred from the native language.

For this reason, differences in ordering of sentence constituents like subject and predicate, for example, would lead to more serious errors than the ordering of smaller constituents of either subject or predicate. If our hierarchy is to be meaningful, it will have to be arranged in terms of all components of language and account for the different domains of each realization language-specific rule. Brière (1968) questions the application of linguistic constructs to determine a hierarchy of difficulty. We must, however, distinguish between contrast and interference. What we have said about the differences between two languages has been cast in terms of theories of competence. To predict interference, the teacher is dealing not only with competence (and our formal list of contrasts) but also with performance factors.

8.3 The Audiolingual Skills

An integral part of the audiolingual theory of language instruction is the partition of language performance into four areas: aural comprehension, speaking, reading, and writing. What is even more important for the theory is that these areas are usually ranked in terms of their priority in instruction. Thus, aural comprehension is considered prior to speaking with respect to instructional focus. Speaking comes next and reading and writing are left to be emphasized on the more advanced levels. Audiolingual materials are often organized so that comprehension and speaking are stressed during the early stages with exercises in reading and writing coming later on. When a student is able to perform well according to a value judgement of the instructor, or according to some predetermined norm, he is said to have developed a 'skill.' The desired goal, of course, is to have him develop the skills of a native speaker of the language. There are other ways to group these skills. Bruner (1966; p.102), for example, points out that there is an important difference between deciphering (listening and reading) and enciphering (speaking and writing). The latter skills are far more demanding than the former. He writes that it is easiest to fall asleep reading, next most easy listening, and only with difficulty while writing or speaking. If degree of involvement in the communication process is a factor, there is no reason why one should not approach the listening and reading skills as a group and speaking and writing as another.

A serious problem, of course, is determining what should be meant by comprehension. Just what decoding process is involved? Some audiolingual teachers will exhort their students to "think in the target language," and not to translate. If translation is the process whereby articulated utterances are broken down into their component parts and then reassembled in another language, we can assume that the teacher hopes that the students will not go through this laborious process in learning to speak the target language. Trying to provide a clear definition of "thinking in a foreign language" is quite another matter. Surely the teacher can't mean not to employ the rules which are shared by both native and target language. As we have seen in this book, languages share many rules. The only linguistic analogue that we can propose to thought is the disposition of the speaker-hearer to utilize the components of the target language as if he did not know any other language. It remains to be proven that such a disposition is possible short of aphasia. A more modest proposal to make to the teacher is to keep the semantic references as close as possible to those of the target language. In this way the student finds himself needing to communicate about situations which are new and/or strange to him, together with those which are necessarily shared in the culture to which he belongs.

We must also recognize that the ranking of audiolingual skills with writing last is due in no small part to the emphasis audiolingualists have placed on the spoken word. Another factor is our comparative ignorance of what mental processes relate to reading. Perhaps we would be on safer ground if we spoke only of deciphering and enciphering skills, with comprehension basic to all of them.

Deciphering	*Enciphering*
listening	speaking
reading	writing

Such a division would allow the teacher more freedom in devising techniques to fit the various writing systems that languages employ. In some languages, the written symbols are correlated to sounds. In others, the correlation is largely one of symbol to morpheme. English writing mixes features of both types:

1. symbol to sound: *pin* as opposed to *bin*
2. symbol to morpheme: *two, too, to* or *sight, site*

As Moulton (1966; p.117) has so succinctly put it: "[writing] is a method of reminding us on paper of things we already know how to say."

Since enciphering and deciphering, involving either the spoken or the written word, are intimately connected and impossible to teach separately, the only reason for focussing on, say, listening and speaking is one of preference. There appears to be no empirical reason why reading and writing skills could not be developed almost from the start, along with the other two. Indeed some audiolingual programs can be criticized in their lack of concern to produce literate students of foreign languages who can hold their own in reading and writing scientific or literary prose.

8.4 The Writing of Exercises

Once a determination has been made of the ways in which the target language differs from the native language of the student, any number of exercises can be built around the differences. We have grouped them under the following headings:

1. substitution types
2. pattern transformations
3. deep-to-surface realizations
4. parsing (decomposition)
5. translation
6. situation drills

Substitution types are often used with regard to vocabulary. A *frame sentence* may be given, such as:

Quant à moi, je n'aime pas *les tomates*.

The students are then instructed to substitute other words or phrases for the part of the sentence which is underlined or italicized (*les tomates*). If the teacher wishes to build a competence in vocabulary which derive from related semantic fields, the words to be substituted can be so limited: *les haricots verts, les épinards,* etc. and the students are led to say: *Quant à moi, je n'aime pas les haricots verts,* and so on. The teacher may have the students do the exercise in chorus or individually or in different sized groupings. Also, the teacher may require the student to supply the item to be substituted. However it is varied, the exercise is of the substitution type as long as the student is not required to change the structure in some way.

A number of different substitutions may be made at different intervals, or in different parts of the frame sentence, as in the following:

Frame sentence and first

Substitution:	Roberto va *alla stazione.*
	al cinema.
Students:	Roberto va al cinema.
Substitution:	*Maria.*
Students:	Maria va al cinema.
Substitution:	*corre*
Students:	Maria corre al cinema.

And so on.

Substitution type exercises can also be used to present conjugation patterns:

Frame sentence (for person):	Hans geht nach Berlin.
Substitution:	*Hans und Fritz.*
Students:	Hans und Fritz gehen nach Berlin.
Frame sentence (for tense):	Hans geht nach Berlin.
Substitution:	*ging*
Students:	Hans ging nach Berlin.

And so on.

Pattern transformation exercises are those in which the teacher interrelates surface patterns via some sort of transformational operation. Questions, for example, may be built from declaratives:

Base sentence:	Paris est loin d'ici.
Prefix expression:	Est-ce que
Students:	Est-ce que Paris est loin d'ici?

In a variation of pattern transformation, base sentences are the recipients of embedded sentences:

Base sentence:	Me gusta mucho.
Embedded sentence:	Este vino es de España.
Result:	Me gusta mucho este vino de España.

As yet another variation, two base sentences may be conjoined by some explicit operation, as in:

Base sentence no. 1:	Preferisco starmene a casa.
Base sentence no. 2:	Non ho soldi per viaggiare.
Instruction:	Join (2) to (1) with *perchè*:
Result:	Preferisco starmene a casa perchè non ho soldi per viaggiare.

Or, the operation may be reversed and the student required to break a sentence with embeddings or a conjoined sentence down into its components, e.g.; Ci si mette tanto tempo per arrivare lì perchè non ci sono treni in coincidenza.

which breaks down into:

1. Ci si mette tanto tempo per arrivare lì.
2. Non ci sono treni in coincidenza.

Both deep-to-surface realizations and parsing are rule-oriented. The rules are essentially those taken from the model of competence. Thus, the student may be asked to realize a deep-structure tree (Figure 8.1) in French, making *Charles* the subject of the surface sentence:

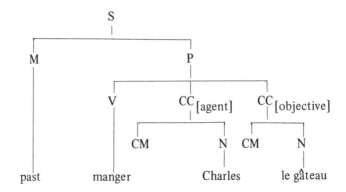

Figure 8.1 Deep structure tree to be realized in French

If the student has been taught the rules in some explicit way, he will be able to produce: *Charles a mangé le gâteau.* If the teacher does not wish to use tree diagrams, the same goal can be achieved by asking the student to form sentences in which *Charles*, as agent, is subject and *le gâteau*, as objective, is object, and so on. Actually, this is a very old technique in language teaching. Those readers familiar with the grammar translation method will recall reference being made to logical subject, for example. Parsing is also a long-used technique. Along with explicit rule giving, it has fallen into disfavor with audiolingualists. Our own opinions are given below in section 5 of this chapter. Basically, parsing involves the analysis of sentences in the target language according to explicit grammatical rules. The student might be asked to give a grammatical definition to parts of various sentences, or draw tree diagrams showing the relationships of sentence parts. The teacher might ask, for example:

1. What is the agent in the following sentence?
2. Is the modality past or present?

   Sentence: On a eu de la chance.

Translation exercises can range from requiring literal renderings from the target to the native language to commentary in the native language about the sentence. An example of the former is as follows:

Translate: Charles est un homme grand.
                              Charles est un grand homme.
                              (to show the difference in meaning
                              which comes with adjective positioning).

Or, the student may be given a sentence like: *Hay mucha nieve en las sierras* and be asked to say whether it would be appropriate for skiing, swimming, or boating. The teacher may wish to give a sentence in the student's native language and have him translate it. However it is done, translation can be as structured as any of the other exercises.

In the use of situation drills, an effort is made to involve the student personally in the messages of the language. It is believed that learning will be enhanced if the student must utilize the target language to describe a situation in which he finds himself or to express a conclusion based on some data which has been presented to him. In teaching the expression of aspect in English to speakers of French, for example, the teacher is faced with getting across the use of the so-called progressive forms of the English verb. Where the French speaker may say only:

J'ouvre la fenêtre.

he finds himself faced with the necessity to distinguish in English between:

I open the window.   *and*   I am opening the window.

To introduce the situation drill, the teacher may first wish to explain the differences formally or even engage the students in some kind of pattern practice or substitution exercise. When the teacher believes that sufficient preparation has been made, one of the students is asked to open a window. As he is engaged in this activity, the teacher says to him:

What are you doing?

If the reply is the correct one *(I am opening the window)*, the teacher proceeds to put the other students through similar activities (opening the door, picking up the book, etc.). Immediate correction is made whenever the reply is wrong.

Related to the situation drill is the type in which data or information is manipulated by the students. As in the illustration given above, the grammatical background is prepared by some sort of exercise, drill, or explanation. Different features of language can be focused upon. Let us consider briefly the area of semantics. In contrast to the English expressions of family relationships *nephew, niece, grandson,* and *granddaughter,* Italian uses only *nipote* (there is an alternant, *nipotino/nipotina* for *grandson* and *granddaughter,* but it need not concern us here). In exposing the Italian-speaking student to the many expressions in English, the teacher may make use of a make-believe geneological tree diagram, as in Figure 8.2.

Referring to the diagram, the teacher can then ask questions such as:

What relation is Tommy to Peter?   Who is Henry's neice?
Who is Mary's grandson?

The questions may even be put in terms of fill-ins:

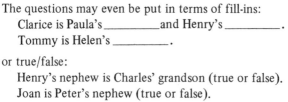

Clarice is Paula's_____and Henry's_____.

Tommy is Helen's_____.

or true/false:

Henry's nephew is Charles' grandson (true or false).

Joan is Peter's nephew (true or false).

That is, a number of questions can be asked to lead the Italian-speaking student of English to utilize terms which have no direct counterparts in his native language.

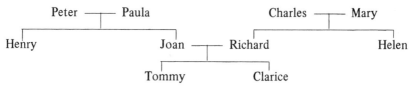

Figure 8.2   Geneological tree diagram

We shall not go into further detail about how exercises can be written. If the reader wishes to pursue the matter further, there are a number of books which he can consult (Lado, 1964; Politzer, 1965; Rivers, 1968; etc.). It is most important for the reader to keep in mind that these exercises may be presented in any number of ways to promote learning of both deciphering and enciphering skills, with either the written or the spoken word.

8.5 Building Competence Drive

Aside from ascertaining the goal of instruction (in our case, the model of language competence), the greatest task any teacher has, is that of motivating the student to learn. According to Bruner (1966), classroom or laboratory activity need not be interpreted only as preparation for later application of what has been taught to 'real' situations. Instead, what is done in the program of instruction can be looked upon as promoting the motivation to learn, or, in Bruner's terms, the building of a 'competence drive.' No matter how detailed or how carefully structured a program may be, if it does not motivate the student to learn, it is useless. As teachers commonly know, more than just the program of instruction is involved. If either the teacher or the students are not responsive to it, competence drive will not be built. The best of instructional programs can become like the charge of the light brigade: magnificent but totally irrelevant!

If Bruner is correct in his interpretation of the need to build competence, we cannot delude ourselves that the devices we use as language teachers will automatically create in the student spontaneous choices of the type that student would make in the normal use of language. Instruction is a game that we play with the hope that the student will learn and be able to transfer this learning to circumstances meaningful to him. The use of grammatical rules in language teaching has been discredited on the grounds that they do not lend themselves readily to the needs of communication. But, we might ask ourselves, are dialogues in which the student is forced to play roles totally alien to his own needs much more transferable? What analogue to the communicational use of language can we find in the substitution drill or in the manipulation of surface patterns? Even if we claim that our audiolingual method uses the spoken word, can we also guarantee that our students will use this word to express what they actually feel? One student told me that, as a result of a dialogue set in a restaurant, she could order a meal much as a native speaker would. But, she confided to me, she still wouldn't know what she was ordering or even if she would like the food. If the dialogue had been a success, she might have been motivated to look up the dishes given on the 'play' menu in a gastronomic encyclopedia, or even seek out a restaurant specializing in the foods of that country. The point is that if the student is not motivated to continue learning, the most carefully planned program is a failure. The reader should not, however, conclude that exercises are useless. Effectively employed, exercises lead the student to learn the language and do not become ends in themselves. The student should not be led to believe that the exercises and dialogues themselves are the goals of our instruction. A good grade should not be given just because the student has learned to manipulate all the drills and exercises in a mechanical way.

Those teachers who employ wide variability or diverse techniques in their instruction have, I believe, an insight into the problem of building and sustaining competence drive (see Hall, 1968). Seen in this light, variability pertains only to the use of instructional devices and not to the model of competence. Regardless of how varied the teacher makes his approach, the model of language competence—the theoretical framework which the student is building—cannot be varied lest an incorrect one be learned. Each one of the contrastive points between native and target language can be presented in a variety of ways—and the teacher would be wise to employ different techniques in order to assure continuing interest on the part of the student. There are teachers whose approach differs from day to day thereby keeping the students interested in what is coming next. Yet even variation is useless if the students are not motivated to learn by it— and they will not be if they have become accustomed to approaches which do not vary.

There is much research to be done on what instructional devices are most conducive to competence drive. Apparently there are many factors relating not only to the student's age, sex, and past educational experiences but also to the teacher's. It has been painful for many teachers trained in a grammar/translation approach to convert themselves to the more recent audiolingual approach. One can only guess at how much has been sacrificed with regard to the teacher's own repertoire of devices for motivating students because of a shift to a less familiar approach. Now that an entire generation of teachers trained in audiolingualism is growing up, the shift to the overt teaching of rules would be just as difficult. In this seventh decade of the twentieth century we have started to understand the development of cognition in the individual. Psychologists tell us that there are many types of learning processes and that they develop at different times as the individual matures. It will be of great use to the language teacher to know, for example, at what age patterned oral responses work best and when the giving of explicit rules is most appropriate. When a sufficient number of factors are known not only about age but about all the rest, we will be able to move toward an individualization of language instruction which will put the optimum stress on competence drive.

The teacher will do well to recognize that he is not always in control of the learning that is going on in the classroom. Since every speech act contains elements of semantics, syntax, and phonology occurring simultaneously, devices that emphasize one particular feature cannot help but entail many others. Thus, substitution frames involve more than just vocabulary learning—they also carry with them a particular syntactic arrangement and many features of pronunciation. To explain the gratuitous acquisition of such features, one speaks of *overlearning*.

There is yet another, more purposeful application of this principle of overlearning that could be termed the *subversive* technique. If desired, the teacher may purposefully shift the focus away from the point to be learned by burying it in the framework of the exercise. Teaching the use of the subjunctive after *il faut que* in French, for example, can be facilitated by using the expression with a verb in a substitution of vocabulary, e.g.,

Teacher: Il faut que vous alliez *à la gare.*
Teacher (cue): *à l'école.*

Students:	Il faut que vous alliez à l'école.
Teacher (cue):	*à l'hôtel.*
Students:	Il faut que vous alliez à l'hôtel.

And so on.

The overt purpose of this device is to teach vocabulary and, perhaps, use of the preposition *à* for direction. The student, however, is also exposed to the subjunctive. Some teachers even recommend subversive techniques in order to teach contrasts in the target language which have no counterparts in the native language. Roger Hadlich (1965), for example, points out that by not overtly contrasting lexical items like *saber* and *conocer, ser* and *estar* in Spanish for English speaking learners, these items were learned without the students aware that there was a problem. It is unfortunate that teachers have sometimes misunderstood the purpose of CA. Once we uncover the contrasts, they need not be presented in contrasting sets. In fact, presenting them in contrasting sets may even be conducive to error-making. In a word, CA tells us what needs to be covered, not how it should be covered.

A chapter on language instruction would not be very useful without a word about testing. As others have pointed out (e.g., Lado, 1961), a test is a teaching device. Without a doubt, a test can serve as an efficient way to motivate the students. There are several kinds of tests (e.g., aptitude, diagnostic, achievement), and the achievement type is the one which concerns us most here. The test items themselves can follow closely the organization of the exercises. In this way, the student is not faced with strange procedures. In important ways, however, even tests can fall short of their intended purpose. Tests have become very much a part of our western civilization, and it is easy to fall into the habit of considering them ends in themselves. It is a known fact that students can 'study for a test,' pass it and leave the course having missed the real goal of instruction. Children who come from cultures where tests are not overtly given often do badly on western type tests, regardless of their aptitude. Even children from the lower economic classes of western society may do poorly in tests and thereby be assigned low IQs. In language work, the most appropriate test is the one which evaluates the learner's actual performance in a real situation. Unfortunately such tests are not easily quantifiable. (For an example of tests which approximate the communicational situation, see those given by the Foreign Service Institute of the U.S. Department of State.)

There is yet another way in which tests are unreliable as a way to gauge achievement. When we give a formal test, we are eliciting one set of performances. Thus, if we give only a few formal tests throughout the course of instruction, we are not getting a real idea of how well the student can speak or read or write the language, or, in other words, how competent he has become in the language. The only way out of this dilemma is to test our students daily—and do it through conversation and writing. We must remember that no single test can tell the teacher more about the student's achievement than what the teacher already knows by daily contact with the student.

Some criticism has been made of the use of contrastive data in classes where the students are of different language backgrounds (see, for example, Ratmell, 1969). Such is often the case in the teaching of English to speakers of other languages in the United States. While cognizant of the need to do so, we can only conclude that mixed classes are not really the most conducive to developing a model of competence. Some exercises are bound to be irrelevant for some students while critical for others. One way to avoid this problem would be to prepare tapes and special exercises directed to certain language backgrounds which can accompany other parts of the instruction. Of great aid to the student in such situations is the fact that he is in a country where the language of general communication is the one he is studying. This serves to offset the redundancies of instruction (see Becica, 1969, for application of CA in heterolinguistic classes).

Foreign language teachers are periodically charged with the task of choosing a new textbook. Among the many factors to consider are (1) the variety of exercises, (2) the appropriateness of the contexts around which the exercises are built, and (3) the approach to and coverage of grammar. As far as the exercises are concerned, the teacher can use as ready reference the various types illustrated in this chapter. However varied the exercises may be, the most important matter to consider is the extent to which the variation suits the teacher and the potential students. As experienced teachers know, changing the format of exercises in the second or third year of language instruction can have damaging results. A word of caution goes out to the language teacher who finds himself deluged almost yearly with new materials. If a change must be made, it must be somehow a change for the better. The appropriateness of context may be somewhat easier to evaluate than the exercises. How well do the situations of potential communication as they are presented in the text correspond to reality? If the goal of the course is conversational, will the student emerge with some acquaintance of the contexts in which he is likely to find himself using the language? In the case of reading courses, is the spread of material representative of what the student is likely to read? Are levels of style, both written and oral, represented in any way? Unfortunately, few foreign language texts cover style in a comprehensive way. Understanding the importance of CA and having some conception of language organization will help the teacher to evaluate the grammatical coverage. The textbook should reveal some formal orientation to a theory of language. Parts of speech should be covered systematically, with the differences between native and target language treated either overtly or covertly—but with care. The grammatical orientation should be such that the student can sense the underlying harmony of the language's structure.

In concluding, we exhort the teacher to be enthusiastic himself about all aspects of his profession. None of the teaching devices nor the contrasts between native and target language will be useful if the teacher does not enjoy and believe in what he is doing. Our intention in writing this book has been to provide the teacher with some ideas and information the value of which comes only in application. It is for this reason that we cannot afford to be doctrinaire either about our linguistics or our language teaching.

One final thought. Charles C. Fries (1963; p.215) remarked: "learning to read has no end." That remark could be extended to all of language. We are, for our entire lives, students of language—if not of a foreign one, of our own.

8.6 Problems

1. In what senses, both literal and metaphorical, can we understand the dictum that "learning is child's play"?

2. In the context of the discussion of this chapter, discuss the following excerpt from *How the French Boy Learns to Write*, by Rollo Walter Brown (1963; p. 170):

> But what effect has this method [i.e., the "direct method"], however successful it may be in the teaching of a foreign tongue, on the pupil's speech and writing in his native language? This is the question of the moment to the American teacher of English; and concerning this question there is no unanimity of opinion in France today. By some it is thought that the method has worked absolute harm in this respect. Their argument is (1) that the French boy, however skillfully he may write today, does not write so well as he did formerly; and (2) that the falling off is to be attributed to the "direct method;" inasmuch as it deprives the boy of most of his former practice of translating into his own tongue and obliges him for one or two hours a day to think, speak, and live wholly in the language of another people.

3. Contrast the above excerpt with the following from Foresti (1882; p. x., Preface):

> ... but the method of which I am speaking [i.e., the "classical" or "grammar/translation" method] can never afford this advantage [i.e., the satisfaction of expressing our own thoughts and feelings in a novel way] but in the slightest degree, as a slowly-piled, granite-faced Cyclopean substructure of grammatical rules is considered an indispensable pre-liminary to any attempt at speaking. And while the student reluctantly submits his understanding and memory to the task of encountering these barren formulas and abstract rules, he is never called to make an attempt to connect the sound of his written though rarely spoken words, with the objects to which they belong; but instead thereof is obliged to work out the connection in the slowest and most painful manner possible, by means of his mother tongue and a dictionary.

4. The following are portions of the table of contents taken from two hypothetical texts. The grammatical coverage is in approximately the same areas of an imaginary language. In what ways are the headings suggestive of how the grammar is to be covered? Which text is more likely to proceed in terms of language universals? Which tends to consider surface patterns independently of underlying structure?

A		B	
Chapter	Subject Matter	Chapter	Subject Matter
I	Animate Nouns Verbs of Motion	I	Class I Words Words with *-nung* affix
II	Nouns denoting shape Reiterative Verbs	II	Class II Words with *ab-* prefix Words with *-ix-* infix
III	Inanimate Nouns Expressions of location, agent and objective	III	Class III Words The markers *ge-*, *hi-*, *mo-*
IV	Questions requiring simple affirmation or negation	IV	The use of the expression *bib*

5. Select a language text in which the exercises focus predominantly on surface patterns. What rules can be formulated to interrelate any of the patterns? Does the text account in any way for surface ambiguities?

6. Should translation be considered a fifth 'skill'? How would it fit in with Bruner's classification of the four audiolingual skills?

7. Construct some exercises to teach the use of the passive in English to speakers of French.

8.7 Notes

1. Several recent attempts have been made to delimit the role of interference in foreign language learning. Sciarone (1970; p.131), for example, suggests that the influence of the native language diminishes as the student builds a familiarity with the target language. In other words, the learning of unfamiliar structures and patterns in late stages may not be so subject to influence from the native language as learning which goes on early in the program of instruction.

2. Buteau (1970), in studying students' errors in learning French, concludes that determining degree of difficulty must also lead the teacher to consider the learner's potential awareness of contextual clues. The reader may wish to compare Buteau's findings with those of Brière (1968). Cf. remarks on transfer and interference in Chapter 1.

8.8 Background Readings

1. On theory of instruction:
   Bruner 1966
   Di Pietro 1967

2. Trends and surveys:
   Titone 1965
   Valdman 1966

3. Psychology and language teaching:
   Rivers 1964
   Jakobovits 1970

4. On testing:
   Lado 1961
   Valette 1967
   D. Harris 1969

5. Application to specific languages:
   Feldman & Kline 1969 (to Spanish)
   Finocchiaro 1964 (to English)
   Politzer 1960 (to French)
   Politzer 1968 (to German)
   Politzer & Staubach 1961 (to Spanish)

6. General methodology of language teaching:

Belyayev 1964	Lado 1964
Bosco & Di Pietro 1970	Mackey 1965
Brooks 1964	Moulton 1966
Carroll 1963	Politzer 1965
Hall 1966	Rivers 1968
Hughes 1968	Titone 1968

REFERENCES

Abbreviations:

AA   *American Anthropologist.*
FL   *Foundations of Language.*
IJAL   *International Journal of American Linguistics.*
IRAL   *International Review of Applied Linguistics.*
JL   *Journal of Linguistics.*
Lg.   *Language.*
LL   *Language Learning.*
MLJ   *Modern Language Journal.*

Agard, F. and R. Di Pietro, *The Sounds of English and Italian*, The University of Chicago Press, Chicago, 1965.
———, *The Grammatical Structures of English and Italian*, The University of Chicago Press, Chicago, 1965a.
Alatis, J. (ed.), *Georgetown Monograph Series on Languages and Linguistics*, No. 21, Georgetown University Press, Washington, D. C., 1968.
Bach, E., *An Introduction to Transformational Grammars*, Holt, New York, 1964.
———, 'On Some Recurrent Types of Transformations,' *Georgetown Monograph Series on Languages and Linguistics*, No. 18, (C. Kreidler, ed.), (1965), 3-18.
———, 'Nouns and Noun Phrases,' in Bach and Harms, (1968), 91-122.
———, and R. Harms, (eds.), *Universals in Linguistic Theory*, Holt, New York, 1968.
Bar-Hillel, Y., 'Universal Semantics and Philosophy of Language: Quandaries and Prospects,' in *Substance and Structure of Language*, (J. Puhvel, ed.), The University of California Press, Berkeley, (1969), 1-21.
Bausch, K. R., 'Qualité en traduction et linguistique dite "différentielle" ', *Babel* 1, (1970), 1-8.
Becica, B., 'First Language Background As It Affects ESL Teaching,' *TESOL Quarterly* 3, (1969), 349-353.

Belyayev, B., *The Psychology of Teaching Foreign Languages*, Macmillan, New York, 1964.

Berlin, B. and P. Kay, *Basic Color Terms: Their Universality and Evolution*, The University of California Press, Berkeley, 1970.

Bickerton, D., 'Prolegomena to a Linguistic Theory of Metaphor,' *FL* 5, (1969), 34-52.

Bjerke, R., 'A Contrastive Study of Old German and Old Norwegian Kinship Terms,' Supplement to *IJAL* 35, mem. 22. (1969).

Bloch, B., 'Phonemic Overlapping,' *American Speech* 16, (278-284), reprinted in M. Joos, (ed.), *Readings in Linguistics*, American Council of Learned Societies, Washington, D.C., (1941), 93-96.

Bloomfield, L., *Language*, Holt, New York, 1933.

Bolinger, D., 'The Atomization of Meaning,' *Lg.* 41, (1965), 555-573.

–––, *Aspects of Language*, Harcourt, New York, 1968.

Bosco, F. and R. Di Pietro, 'Instructional Strategies: Their Psychological and Linguistic Bases,' *IRAL* 8, (1970), 1-19.

Brière, E., *A Psycholinguistic Study of Phonological Interference*, Mouton, The Hague, 1968.

Brooks, N., *Language and Language Learning Theory and Practice*, Harcourt, New York, 1964.

Brown, R., *How the French Boy Learns to Write*, National Council of Teachers, Champaign, 1963 (first published in 1915 by Harvard University Press).

Bruner, J., *Toward a Theory of Instruction*, Harvard University Press, Cambridge, 1966.

–––, 'Processes of Cognitive Growth: Infancy,' in *The Eighth Annual Report, Center for Cognitive Studies*, Harvard University Press, Cambridge, 1967-68.

Bull, W., *Spanish for Teachers: Applied Linguistics*, Ronald Press, New York, 1965.

Buteau, M., 'Students' Errors and the Learning of French as a Second Language: A Pilot Study,' *IRAL* 8, (1970) 133-145.

Cárdenas, D., *Introducción a una comparación fonológica del español y del inglés*, Center for Applied Linguistics, Washington, D.C., 1960.

Carroll, J.B., *Language, Thought, and Reality*, M.I.T. Press, Cambridge, 1956.

–––, 'Linguistic Relativity, Contrastive Analysis, and Language Learning,' *IRAL* 1, (1963), 1-20.

Casagrande, J., 'Language Universals in Anthropological Perspective' in Greenberg (1963), 279-298.

Chafe, W., 'Language as Symbolization,' *Lg.* 43, (1967), 57-91.

———, (Review of P. Postal), *Aspects of Phonological Theory*, in *Lg.* 46, (1970), 116-124.

———, *Meaning and the Structure of Language*, The University of Chicago Press, Chicago, 1970a.

Chao, Y., 'A Preliminary Study of English Intonation,' in *Studies Presented to Ts'ai Yuan P'ei on His Sixty-Fifth Birthday*, Academia Sinica, Peiping, 1933.

Chomsky, N., *Syntactic Structures*, Mouton, The Hague, 1957.

———, *Aspects of the Theory of Syntax*, M.I.T. Press, Cambridge, 1965.

———, *Language and Mind*, Harcourt, New York, 1968.

———, and M. Halle, *The Sound Pattern of English*, Harper, New York, 1968.

Companys, E., *Phonétisme français et phonétisme italien*, Bureau d'Etude et de Liaison pour l'Enseignement du Français dans le Monde, Paris, 1965.

Cook, W., *Introduction to Tagmemic Analysis*, Holt, New York, 1969.

Coseriu, E., 'Pour une sémantique diachronique structurale,' *Travaux de linguistique et de littérature*, l'Université, Strasbourg, 1964.

de Laguna, G., *Speech: Its Function and Development*, Indiana University Press, Bloomington, 1963.

Delattre, P., 'Research Techniques for Phonetic Comparison of Languages,' *IRAL* 1, (1963), 85-97.

———, and C. Olsen, 'Syllabic Features and Phonic Impression in English, German, French and Spanish, *Lingua* 22, (1969), 160-175.

Del Olmo, G., 'Professional and Pragmatic Perspectives on the Audiolingual Approach,' *FL Annals* 2, (1968), 19-29.

Dingwall, W., 'Transformational Generative Grammar and Contrastive Analysis,' *LL* 14, (1964), 147-160.

Dinneen, F., *An Introduction to General Linguistics*, Holt, New York, 1966.

Di Pietro, R., 'Separating Noun-Adjective Classes: A Basis for Contrastive Analysis,' *LL* 12, (1963), 303-306.

———, 'Operational and Taxonomic Models in Language Learning,' in *On Teaching English to Speakers of Other Languages*, Series III, (B. J. Robinett, ed.), Teachers of English to Speakers of Other Languages, Washington, D. C., 1967.

———, 'Contrastive Analysis and Notions of Deep and Surface Grammar,' in Alatis (1968), 65-80.

———, 'Competence and Performance in ESL, *TESOL Quarterly* 4, (1970), 49-62.

Dulsey, B., 'Gender Differences in Romance Language Cognates,' *Hispania*, 39, (1956), 466-467.

Feldman, D., and W. Kline, *Spanish: Contemporary Methodology*, Blaisdell, Waltham, 1969.

Ferguson, C., and W. Stewart (eds.), *Linguistic Reading Lists for Teachers of Modern Languages*, Center for Applied Linguistics, Washington, D.C., 1963.

Filipović, R., (ed.), *Reports and Studies, Yugoslav Serbo-Croatian-English Contrastive Project*, Institute of Linguistics, Zagreb, 1970.

Fillmore, C., 'The Case for Case,' in Bach and Harms (1968), 1-88.

Finocchiaro, M., *English as a Second Language: From Theory to Practice*, Regents, New York, 1964.

Fodor, J., and J. Katz, (eds.), *The Structure of Language*, Prentice-Hall, Englewood Cliffs, 1964.

Foresti, F., *Ollendorff's New Method of Learning to Read, Write, and Speak the Italian Language*, Appleton, New York, 1882.

Friedrich, P., 'Shape in Grammar,' *Lg.*, 46, (1970), 379-407.

Fries, C., *Linguistics and Reading*, Holt, New York, 1963.

———, and K. Pike, 'Co-existent Phonemic Systems,' *Lg.* 25, (1949), 29-50.

Gage, W., *Contrastive Studies in Linguistics*, Center for Applied Linguistics, Washington, D.C., 1961.

———, *The Sounds of English and Russian; The Grammatical Structures of English and Russian*, ERIC, Center for Applied Linguistics, Washington, D.C., (unpublished).

Gleason, H., 'Contrastive Analysis and Discourse Structure,' in Alatis (1968), 39-63.

Goldin, M., *Spanish Case and Function*, Georgetown University Press, Washington, D.C., 1968.

Goodenough, W., 'A Problem in Componential Analysis,' *AA* 67, part 2, (1965), 259-287.

Grandgent, C., *German and English Sounds*, Ginn, Boston, 1892.

Greenberg, J., (ed.), *Universals of Language*, second edition, M.I.T. Press, Cambridge, 1966.

———, 'The First (And Perhaps Only) Nonlinguistic Distinctive Feature Analysis,' *Word* 23, (1967), 214-220.

Grevisse, M., *Le bon usage*, Sixième édition, J. Duculot, Gembloux, Belgium, 1955.

Hadlich, R., 'Lexical Contrastive Analysis,' *MLJ* 49, (1965), 426-429.

Hall, R., Jr., *New Ways to Learn a Foreign Language*, Bantam, New York, 1966.

———, 'Contrastive Grammar and Textbook Structure,' in Alatis (1968), 175-183.

Halliday, M.A.K., A. McIntosh, and P. Strevens, *The Linguistic Sciences and Language Teaching*, Indiana University Press, Bloomington, 1964.

Hammer, J., and F. Rice, *A Bibliography of Contrastive Linguistics*, Center for Applied Linguistics, Washington, D.C., 1965.

Harms, R., *Introduction to Phonological Theory*, Prentice-Hall, Englewood Cliffs, 1968.

Harris, D., *Testing English as a Second Language*, McGraw-Hill, New York, 1969.

Harris, Z., 'Transfer Grammar,' *IJAL* 20, (1954), 259-270.

———, *Mathematical Structures of Language*, Interscience, New York, 1968.

Hockett, C., *A Manual of Phonology*, Waverly Press, Baltimore, 1955.

———, *A Course in Modern Linguistics*, Macmillan, New York, 1958.

———, 'Linguistic Elements and Their Relations,' *Lg.* 37, (1961), 29-53.

Hughes, J., *Linguistics and Language Teaching*, Random House, New York, 1968.

Jacobs, R. and P. Rosenbaum, *English Transformational Grammar*, Blaisdell, Waltham, 1968.

Jakobovits, L., *Foreign Language Learning*, Newbury House, Rowley, 1970.

Jakobsen, R. and M. Halle, *Fundamentals of Language*, Mouton, The Hague, 1956.

Joos, M., *The Five Clocks*, Indiana University Press, Bloomington, 1962.

Kaplan, R., 'Contrastive Rhetoric and the Teaching of Composition,' *TESOL Quarterly*, 1, (1967), 10-16.

Katz, J. and J. Fodor, 'The Structure of a Semantic Theory,' *Lg.* 39, (1963), 170-210.

Kessler, A., 'Deep to Surface Contrasts in English and Italian Imperatives,' *LL* 19, (1969), 99-106.

Kiefer, F., *On Emphasis and Word Order in Hungarian*, Indiana University Press, Bloomington, 1967.

Kirkwood, H., 'Translation as a Basis for Contrastive Linguistic Analysis,' *IRAL* 4, (1966), 175-182.

Koutsoudas, A., *Writing Transformational Grammars: An Introduction*, McGraw-Hill, New York, 1966.

Kufner, H., *The Grammatical Structures of English and German*, Chicago University Press, Chicago, 1962.

Kuipers, A., 'Unique Types and Typological Universals,' *Pratidanam*, Mouton, The Hague, 1970.

Ladefoged, P., 'The Nature of General Phonetic Theories,' *Georgetown Monograph Series on Languages and Linguistics*, No. 18 (C. Kreidler, ed.), (1965), 27-42.

Lado, R., *Linguistics Across Cultures*, The University of Michigan Press, Ann Arbor, 1957.

———, *Language Testing. The Construction and Use of FL Tests, A Teacher's Book*, Longmans, London, 1961.

———, *Language Teaching: A Scientific Approach*, McGraw-Hill, New York, 1964.

Lakoff, G., *The Nature of Syntactic Irregularity*, Harvard University Press, Cambridge, 1965.

Lamb, S., 'The Sememic Approach to Structural Semantics,' *AA* 66, (1964), 57-78.

Lampach, S., *Contrastive French Grammar*, ERIC, Center for Applied Linguistics, Washington, D.C., (unpublished).

———, and A. Martinet, *English-French Contrastive Phonology*, ERIC, Center for Applied Linguistics, Washington, D.C., (unpublished).

Langacker, R., *Language and Its Structure*, Harcourt, New York, 1968.

Langendoen, D., *The Study of Syntax*, Holt, New York, 1969.

Leech, G., *Towards a Semantic Description of English*, Indiana University Press, Bloomington, 1970.

Lehrer, A., 'Semantic Cuisine,' *JL* 5, (1969), 39-55.

Lenneberg, E., *Biological Foundations of Language*, Wiley, New York, 1967.

Lisker, L. and A. Abramson, 'A Cross-Language Study of Voicing in Initial Stops: Acoustical Measurement,' *Word* 20, (1964), 384-422.

Longacre, R., 'Some Fundamental Insights of Tagmemics,' *Lg.* 41, (1966), 65-76.

———, *Grammar Discovery Procedures*, Mouton, The Hague, 1968.

Lotz, J., 'Contrastive Study of the Morphophonemics of Obstruent Clusters in English and Hungarian,' in *Miscellanea di studi dedicati a Emerico Várady,* Società editrice Mucchi, Modena, (1966), 197-201.

Lounsbury, F., 'A Formal Account of the Crow- and Omaha-type Kinship Terminologies,' in *Explorations in Cultural Anthropology*, (W. Goodenough, ed.), McGraw-Hill, New York, (1964), 351-393.

Lyons, J., *Structural Semantics*, Blackwell, Oxford, 1963.

———, *Introduction to Theoretical Linguistics*, Cambridge University Press, Cambridge, 1968.

Mackey, W., *Language Teaching Analysis*, Indiana University Press, Bloomington, 1965.

Martinet, A., *Elements of General Linguistics*, University of Chicago Press, Chicago, 1964.

McCawley, J., 'The Role of a Phonological Feature System in a Theory of Language,' *Languages* no. 6, 1967.

———, 'The Role of Semantics in a Grammar,' in Bach and Harms (1968) 125-169.

McNeill, D., 'The Development of Language,' in *Carmichael's Manual of Child Psychology*, (P. A. Mussen, ed.), Wiley, New York, (in press).

Moser, H., (ed.), *Probleme der kontrastiven Grammatick. Jahrbuch 1969.* Schwann, Düsseldorf, 1970.

Moulton, W., *The Sounds of English and German*, The University of Chicago Press, Chicago, 1962.

———, 'Toward a Classification of Pronunciation Errors,' *MLJ* 46, (1962a), 101-109.

———, *A Linguistic Guide to Language Learning*, Modern Language Association of America, New York, 1966.

———, 'The Use of Models in Contrastive Linguistics,' in Alatis (1968), 27-38.

Muljačić, Ž., *Fonologia generale e fonologia della lingua italiana*, Il Mulino, Bologna, 1969.

Neisser, U., *Cognitive Psychology* Appleton, New York, 1967.

Nemser, W., *Hungarian Phonetic Experiments*, American Council of Learned Societies, New York, 1961.

———, 'Contrastive Linguistics at the Center for Applied Linguistics,' *The Linguistic Reporter* 12, (1970), 1-5.

———, and F. Juhasz, *A Contrastive Analysis of Hungarian and English Phonology*, American Council of Learned Societies, New York, 1964.

Nickel, G., (ed.), *PAKS*-Arbeitbericht Nr. 3/4. Universität, Stuttgart, 1969.

Ohannessian, S. and W. Gage, *Teaching English to Speakers of Choctaw, Navajo, and Papago: A Contrastive Approach*, Center for Applied Linguistics, Washington, D.C., 1969.

Passy, P., *Petite phonétique comparée des principales langues européennes.* Paris, 1906.

Pike, K., 'Language as Particle, Wave, and Field,' *Texas Quarterly* 2, (1959), 37-54.

Politzer, R., *Teaching French: A Linguistic Orientation*, Blaisdell, Waltham, 1960.

———, *Foreign Language Learning: A Linguistic Introduction*, Prentice-Hall, Englewood Cliffs, 1965.

———, *Teaching German: A Linguistic Orientation*, Blaisdell, Waltham, 1968.

———, and C. Staubach, *Teaching Spanish: A Linguistic Orientation*, Blaisdell, Waltham, 1961.

Postal, P., 'On So-called 'Pronouns' in English,' in *Georgetown Monograph Series on Languages and Linguistics*, No. 19, (F. P. Dineen, ed.), (1966), 177-206, reprinted in Reibel and Schane (1969), 201-224.

Ratmell, G., 'Homolinguistic vs. Heterolinguistic TESOL Classes,' *TESOL Quarterly* 3, (1969), 51-53.

Reed, D., R. Lado, and Y. Shen, 'The Importance of the Native Language in Foreign Language Learning,' *LL* 1, (1948), 17-23.

Reibel, D., and S. Schane (eds.), *Modern Studies in English*, Prentice-Hall, Englewood Cliffs, 1969.

Ritchie, W., 'On the Explanation of Phonic Interference,' *LL* 28, (1968), 183-197.

Rivers, W., *The Psychologist and the Foreign Language Teacher*, The University of Chicago Press, Chicago, 1964.

———, *Teaching Foreign Language Skills*, The University of Chicago Press, Chicago, 1968.

Robinson, J., 'Dependency Structures and Transformational Rules,' *Lg.* 46, (1970), 259-285.

Rosen, R., 'Heirarchical Organization in Automata Theoretic Models of the Central Nervous System,' in *Information Processing in the Nervous System*, (K. Leibovic, ed.), Springer-Verlag, New York, (1969), 21-34.

Ross, J., 'On the Cyclic Nature of English Pronominalization,' in *To Honor Roman Jakobson*, Mouton, The Hague, (1967), p. 1669-1682, (reprinted in Reibel and Schane, 1969).

———, 'Adjectives as Noun Phrases,' in Reibel and Schane (1969), 352-360.

Rutherford, W., 'Deep and Surface Structure and the Language Drill,' *TESOL Quarterly* 2, (1968), 71-79.

Saltarelli, M., 'Spanish Plural Formation: Apocope or Epenthesis,' *Lg.* 46, (1970), 89-96.

Saporta, S., 'Applied Linguistics and Generative Grammar,' in Valdman (1966), 81-92.

Schachter, P., *A Contrastive Analysis of English and Pangasian*, (Ph.D. Dissertation), UCLA Press, Los Angeles, 1960.

Schane, S., 'L'élision et la liaison en français,' *Languages* 8, (1967), 37-59.

Sciarone, A., 'Contrastive Analysis—Possibilities and Limitations,' *IRAL* 8, (1970), 115-131.

Selinker, L., *A Psycholinguistic Study of Language Transfer*, (Ph.D. Dissertation), Georgetown University, Washington, D.C., 1966.

Shen, Y., 'Linguistic Experience and Linguistic Habit,' *LL* 12, (1962), 133-150.

Slobin, D. (ed.), *A Field Manual for Cross-cultural Study of the Acquisition of Communicative Competence*, The University of California Press, Berkeley, 1967.

Sokolov, Y., *Perception and the Conditioned Reflex*, Macmillan, New York, 1963.

Stockwell, R., *A Contrastive Analysis of English and Tagalog*, (unpublished).

———, 'Contrastive Analysis and Lapsed Time,' in Alatis (1968), 11-26.

———, and J. Bowen, *The Sounds of English and Spanish*, The University of Chicago Press, Chicago, 1965.

———, J. Bowen, and J. Martin, *The Grammatical Structures of English and Spanish*, The University of Chicago Press, Chicago, 1965.

Suci, G., 'Relations Between Semantic and Syntactic Factors in the Understanding of Language,' *Language and Speech* 12, (1969), 69-79.

Titone, R., *Le lingue estere: metodologia didattica*, PAS-Verlag, Rome, 1965.

———, *Teaching Foreign Languages: An Historical Sketch*, Georgetown University Press, Washington, D.C., 1968.

Tyler, S. (ed.), *Cognitive Anthropology*, Holt, New York, 1969.

Valdman, A., (ed.), *Trends in Language Teaching*, McGraw-Hill, New York, 1966.

Valette, R., *Modern Language Testing*, Harcourt, New York, 1967.

Viëtor, W., *Elemente der Phonetik des Deutschen, Englischen und Franzosischen*, Leipzig, 1894.

Wardhaugh, R., 'Three Approaches to Contrastive Phonological Analysis,' *Canadian Journal of linguistics* 13, (1967), 3-14.

———, 'The Contrastive Analysis Hypothesis,' Fourth Annual TESOL Convention, San Francisco, (1970), published in *TESOL Quarterly* 4, (1970), 123-130.

Weinreich, U., *Languages in Contact*, Linguistic Circle of New York, New York, 1953.

Whorf, B., 'Languages and Logic,' *Technology Review*, M.I.T., 1941, reprinted in *Language, Thought, and Reality*, (J. B. Carroll, ed.), M.I.T. Press, 1956.

Wolff, H., 'Partial Comparisons of the Sound Systems of English and Puerto-Rican Spanish,' *LL* 3, (1950), 38-41.

INDEX

accent, xii
accusative, 71 (see also, case category)
acoustic correlates, 157
active and passive, 5, 63, 75; transformations 47-8; in Arabic, French, Japanese, Spanish, 76ff.
adjectives, 88-93, 107 (note), 108; and nouns, 89-90; and verbs, 88-90
adverbs, 107 (note); formation of, 129
Agard, F., xiv, 11, 31, 158 (see also, Di Pietro)
alpha convention, 145
Altaic, xiii
ambiguous surface structure, 25, 26
anaphora, 98
anomia, 23
anthropologists, cognitive, 58
antonymy and synonymy, 134
Apachean, 141
aphasia, 23, 54
Arabic, 29
arbitrariness, 73
article, definite, 94-6; indefinite, 94
articulation, 136
aspect, 14, 122
autonomous descriptive statements, 4 (see also, models)

Bach, E., 14, 33, 39, 51, 53, 54 (see also, Harms, R.)
Bar-Hillel, Y., 134
Bausch, K.-R., 48
Becica, B., 174
Belyayev, B., 178
Berlin, B. and P. Kay, 134
Bickerton, D., 134
bilingualism, 10, 33
Bloomfield, L., 13-4
Bolinger, D., 14, 34, 38, 51, 112, 134
Bosco, F. and R. Di Pietro, 178
Bowen, J., 11, 12, 31 (see also, Stockwell)
Brière, E.,6-7 (see also, interference);164,177
Brooks, N., 178
Brown, R., 175
Bruner, J., 57, 71, 159, 164, 170ff., 177
Bull, W., 160
Buteau, M., 177

Cárdenas, D., xiv
Carroll, J., 178

Casagrande, J., 133
case category, 40, 55-6, 60ff.; frames, 64; marker, 56, 60ff., 82; realization of, 82; relationships, 64; deep and surface, 71
cases, 54
Center for Applied Linguistics, xiv
Chafe, W., 51, 130, 138
Chao, Y., 10
children's speech, 23
Chinese, 64; contrasted with English, 7-8, 29-31, 107 (see also, Mandarin Chinese)
Choctaw, xiv
Chomsky, N., 11, 25, 28, 45, 58-9; and M. Halle, xii, 2, 38, 39, 51, 136, 137, 144, 157, 158
choosing a textbook, 174-5
color terms, 134
Companys, E., 158
competence, 20; and performance, 19-22
competence drive, 159ff.; building of, 170-4
complementary distribution, 139
conjunction, 105-6
contoid, 55
contrast and interference, 164
contrastive analysis, background notes, 9-14; definition, 2; developments in, 1-14; directions, 12, 13; evaluation of output, 32; general remarks, 2-5; motivation, 1; procedures for, 28-31; theory and procedures, 15-33; translation as a basis for, 48-9
contrastive studies series (see, Center for Applied Linguistics)
convergent or divergent, 6
Cook, W., 14
copula, 81-2; in Chinese, English, French, German, Italian, Korean, Russian, Spanish, 85ff.
Coseriu, E., 133
criteria for evaluating, 5
cultural systems, xii

dative, 64, 71; in German, 83 (see also, case category, and, Fillmore's dative)
decompositional contexts, 112, 114, 121; process, 118
deep structure, 23-7, 74ff.; and surface, 5, 106 (see also, deep-to-surface dimension)
deep-to-surface dimension, 36, 45, 47 (see also, exercises, and, language design)